The Retirement Researcher's Guide Series

Reverse Mortgages

How to Use Reverse Mortgages to Secure Your Retirement

Third Edition

With 2023 Updates

Wade D. Pfau, PhD, CFA, RICP

Published by Retirement Researcher Media, Vienna, Virginia.

Library of Congress Cataloging-in-Publication Data:

Pfau, Wade Donald, 1977–

Reverse Mortgages: How to Use Reverse Mortgages to Secure Your Retirement / Wade Donald Pfau.

pages cm

Includes index.

ISBN [978-1-945640-12-4] (paperback) - ISBN [978-1-945640-13-1] (e-book) - ISBN [978-1-945640-14-8] (hardcover)

Library of Congress Control Number: 2022903289

Retirement Researcher, Vienna, VIRGINIA

1. Retirement Planning. 2. Financial, Personal. I. Title.

Cover Design: Trevor Alexander

Printed in the United States of America

To my family

Table of Contents

Preface

Reverse mortgages are an important tool in the retirement income toolkit. As a professor of retirement income, I meant to investigate them more carefully for a long time. I suppose they did not quickly rise to the top of my to-do list because of the conventional wisdom that they are generally expensive and only worthwhile if everything else has failed. In the fall of 2014, I began to learn more about reverse mortgages and quickly found them to be a fascinating and misunderstood financial product.

In isolation, reverse mortgages can look expensive. One might question the motivations of researchers who argue that reverse mortgages can add value to a retirement plan. But reverse mortgages should not be viewed in isolation. We need to focus on their overall contribution and interactions with other retirement assets.

Retirement is different from what people are accustomed to when working. Risks change. Retirees must sustain spending while managing unknown longevity, as sequence-of-return risk amplifies the impacts of investment volatility, and as unexpected spending shocks require additional liquid funds not already earmarked for other purposes.

Reverse mortgage costs can be offset by gains elsewhere in the financial plan as they help to manage these retirement risks. The value of the reverse mortgage can mostly be found in its ability to create more diversification for investment assets in retirement. Taking distributions from investments can dig a hole that is hard to recover from, and wise use of a reverse mortgage helps to sustain the investment portfolio in retirement, creating a net positive impact after full consideration of its costs. These points are often missed.

I released the first edition of this book in 2016. At that time, I was writing a comprehensive book about retirement planning. The first edition came about as the chapter being written about housing wealth and reverse mortgages kept growing to the point that it became a standalone book. I finally published that broader retirement book as the *Retirement Planning Guidebook: Navigating the Important Decisions for Retirement Success*. The *Guidebook* provides a summary of this book and covers many more related topics such as spending from investments in retirement, claiming Social Security, and building tax-efficient distribution plans.

Here is what's new in this third edition of *Reverse Mortgages*:

- Case study examples have been entirely redesigned to be based on historical market data instead of Monte Carlo simulations, which I hope will improve their transparency and clarity.

- The case studies now also fully incorporate income tax calculations so that the precise amount of annual taxes can be included without the need for simplifications.
- More intuition about how reverse mortgages can help manage retirement risk is provided throughout the book.
- I use a simple new decision rule for portfolio coordination strategies.
- I have added content about using the HECM to fund Roth conversions.
- Treasury rates have replaced the LIBOR for reverse mortgage calculations.
- There is a new section on proprietary reverse mortgages.
- There is a new section on the growing trend of refinancing a reverse mortgage.
- I include a discussion of the Retirement Income Style Awareness to help summarize the broader picture of retirement planning.

In the last chapter, I provide some suggestions about finding a reverse mortgage lender. One suggestion that I'll add here, and there is no way to say this without sounding smug, but you might ask a potential lender if he or she knows who I am. I may be the only author of a reverse mortgage book who does not work within the reverse mortgage industry. I come at the problem from an outsider's perspective of thinking more broadly about how a reverse mortgage can best fit into an overall retirement plan. Lenders who know of me are more likely to better understand the broader retirement planning picture as well. Since this book's initial release, it has always been neck and neck with Dan Hultquist's excellent *Understanding Reverse* as the best-selling book on reverse mortgages, so it is not unreasonable to expect a reverse mortgage lender to know about this book and its contents.

My overarching interest is in building efficient retirement income plans to support the most spending potential for assets, both during life and as a legacy. My research has led me to conclude that in many cases, reverse mortgages can provide value toward achieving this end. I hope you will find this exploration of the research useful. I welcome your feedback and questions.

You can reach me at **wade@retirementresearcher.com**.

As a final note, I have tried to avoid including footnotes to make the book more readable and give it a less academic feel. At the end of the book, I have included a list for further reading that includes bibliographic information for resources mentioned as well as other helpful resources.

Wade Pfau

Dallas, TX

January 2023

Acknowledgments

Writing a book is a major endeavor, and I have been helped along the way by countless individuals. First and foremost, I would like to thank my colleagues at Retirement Researcher and McLean Asset Management for providing the vision and resources to make this book possible. I am grateful for the leadership and willingness of Alex Murguia and Dean Umemoto to build a firm that turns my retirement income research into practical solutions for real-world retirees. I would also like to thank Trevor Alexander, Brian Bass, Briana Corbin, Rob Cordeau, Bob French, Paula Friedman, Christian Litscher, Morgan Menzies, Stephen Pomanti, Jason Rizkallah, and Jessica Wunder.

Furthermore, I am grateful to the American College of Financial Services for their leadership and focus on retirement income planning, particularly David Blanchett, Michael Finke, George Nichols, Kirk Okumura, Steve Parrish, and Art Prunier.

I am also deeply indebted to Don and Lynne Komai and the Watermark Design Office for inspiring the layout and design for this book.

Next, I wish to thank Shelley Giordano and the Funding Longevity Taskforce (Barry Sacks, Marguerita Cheng, Thomas C. B. Davison, Christopher Mayer, John Salter, and Sandra Timmermann) for sparking my interest and educating me about reverse mortgages and for being a resource to answer my many questions. Extra thanks to Tom Davison for suggesting the book title and providing me with detailed comments on my initial draft. The Taskforce has since evolved into the Academy for Home Equity in Financial Planning at the University of Illinois at Urbana-Champaign, under the leadership of Craig Lemoine, and I'm glad to continue being part of this organization.

The next group of individuals I must thank include many reverse mortgage professionals who have helped me better understand their industry. These include, in alphabetical order: Harlan Accola, Marvis Baehr, Peter Bell, Chuck Berry, Jim Cullen, Joe Damo, David Darling, Tom Dickson, Tom Evans, Don Graves, Christina Harmes, Scott Harmes, Dan Hultquist, Tim Jackson, Todd Jarvis, Darryl Johnson, Elena Katsulos, Jay Kaplan, Vaughn Kavlie, Tim Kennedy, Joe DeMarkey, Rasty Goodwin, Mary Lafaye, Richard MacFadden, Bob Mikelskas, Christian Mills, Scott Norman, Alex Pistone, Colleen Rideout, Jim Spicka, James Stanko, Robert Trommler, Shain Urwin, James Veale, Jim Warns, and Jenny Werwa.

I also wish to thank countless other practitioners, researchers, and readers who have helped me along the way. A partial list must include: Dana

Anspach, Bill Bengen, Bill Bernstein, Jason Branning, Jason Brown, J. Brent Burns, Ian Cahill, Bill Cason, Curtis Cloke, Jeremy Cooper, Wade Dokken, Harold Evensky, Francois Gadenne, Jonathan Guyton, David Jacobs, Dean Harder, Rick Hayes, Jamie Hopkins, Robert Huebscher, Stephen Huxley, Michael Kitces, David Lau, David Littell, Kevin Lyles, Manish Malhotra, Ben Mattlin, Ed McGill, Moshe Milevsky, Aaron Minney, Dan Moisand, Brent Mondoskin, Sheryl Moore, John Olsen, Emilio Pardo, Kerry Pechter, Robert Powell, John M. Prizer Jr., Michelle Richter, Will Robbins, Jason and Art Sanger, Bill Sharpe, Jeff Smith, Larry Swedroe, Tomiko Toland, Joe Tomlinson, Bob Veres, Steve Vernon, and Bruce Wolfe. I also pay tribute to Dirk Cotton and Dick Purcell, who were both important influences on me and have passed away.

I also wish to thank my family for their support and the sacrifices made to help me get this book written.

Finally, I wish to thank everyone who has read and participated at RetirementResearcher.com since 2010.

Funding Longevity Task Force members at the InvestmentNews Retirement Income Summit in April 2017 (left to right): Sandra Timmerman, Tom Davison, Barry Sacks, Wade Pfau, Shelley Giordano, Jamie Hopkins, and Rita Cheng.

Chapter 1: Overview of Retirement Planning

Without the relative stability provided by earnings from employment, retirees must find a way to convert their financial resources into a stream of income that will last the remainder of their lives. Two trends add to the difficulty of this task. First, people are living longer, and those retiring in their sixties must plan to support a longer period of spending. Second, traditional defined-benefit pensions are becoming less common. Pensions once guaranteed lifetime income by pooling risks across a collection of workers, but fewer employees have access to them today. Instead, employees and employers now tend to contribute to various defined-contribution pensions like 401(k)s, where the employee accepts longevity and investment risk and must make investment decisions. 401(k) plans are not pensions in the traditional sense, as they shift the risks and responsibilities to employees.

If you've been saving and accumulating, the question remains what to do with your pot of assets upon reaching retirement. Essentially, if you wish to retire one day, you are increasingly responsible for figuring out how to save during your working years and convert your savings into sustainable income for an ever-lengthening number of retirement years. These are not easy tasks, but they are manageable.

My goal with the Retirement Researcher's Guide Series of books is to help individuals and their financial advisors move along the right path toward building an efficient retirement income strategy. This book focuses specifically on home equity and whether it may be worthwhile to include a reverse mortgage in your retirement income toolkit. I show that reverse mortgages are worthy of consideration because they help to manage the new risks confronting individuals after they leave the labor force and seek to manage their expenses through distributions generated from their assets.

It is important to note from the outset that retirement income planning is still a relatively new field. Wealth management has traditionally focused on accumulating assets without applying further thought to the differences between pre- and post-retirement financial risk. To put it succinctly, retirees experience a reduced capacity to bear financial-market risk compared to when they still earned income. The standard of living for a retiree becomes more vulnerable to permanent harm because of financial-market downturns.

Tools like reverse mortgages get a bad rap because so much of the financial planning conversation is focused on wealth accumulation, and it is easy to miss how things change after retiring.

While it is relatively new, retirement income planning has emerged as a distinct field in the financial-services profession. The financial circumstances facing retirees are not the same as those of pre-retirees. This calls for different approaches from traditional investment advice for wealth accumulation. Reverse mortgages may seem an odd vehicle when considered from an accumulation mind-set, but they can make sense in a retirement income framework.

A mountain-climbing analogy is useful for clarifying the distinction between accumulation and distribution: The goal of climbing a mountain is not just to make it to the top; it is also necessary to get back down. But the skill set required to get down a mountain is not the same as that needed to reach the summit. In fact, an experienced mountain climber knows that going back down is more treacherous and dangerous; because climbers must deal with greater fatigue, they risk falling farther and with greater acceleration when facing a downslope than when facing an upslope. The way our bodies are designed makes going up easier than coming down.

Exhibit 1.1
The Mountain-Climbing Analogy for Retirement

Distribution—the retirement phase, when you are pulling money from your accounts rather than accumulating wealth—is much like descending a mountain. The objective of a retirement saver is not just to make it to the top of the mountain (achieve a wealth-accumulation target), but to make it down the mountain safely and smoothly by spending assets in a sustainable manner. In this retirement income context, the potential role and value of a reverse mortgage might make more sense.

Key Retirement Planning Principles

As I have attempted to summarize this book's key messages and themes, I've found that the following guidelines serve as a manifesto for my approach to retirement income planning. Much of my writing concerns how to implement these guidelines into a retirement income plan.

1. *The risks are different in retirement.* Retirement risk relates to the inability to meet one's financial goals. The three basic risks for retirees are longevity risk, market risk, and spending shocks. Longevity risk relates to not knowing how long you will live, and thus not knowing how long you must make your wealth last. A long life is wonderful, but it is also costlier and a bigger drain on resources. Half of the population will outlive their statistical life expectancy—which is only increasing with scientific progress.

Market risk relates to the possibility that poor market returns deplete available wealth more quickly than anticipated. There are two issues at work. First, retirees simply have less capacity for risk as they are more vulnerable to a reduced standard of living when risks manifest. Retirees face reduced flexibility to earn income in the labor markets to cushion their standard of living from the impact of poor market returns. Those entering retirement are crossing the threshold into an entirely foreign way of living.

Second, market losses in the early years of retirement can disproportionately hurt the sustainability of a retirement spending plan, creating sequence-of-return risk that amplifies the impacts of market volatility. At one time, investments were a place for saving and accumulation. But retirees must try to create an income stream from their existing assets—this puts an important constraint on their investment decisions. Taking distributions amplifies investment risks (market volatility, interest-rate volatility, and credit risk) by increasing the importance of the order of investment returns in retirement.

When spending from a portfolio, the concept of sequence-of-return risk becomes more relevant as portfolio losses early in retirement increase the percentage of remaining assets withdrawn as income. This can dig a hole from which it becomes increasingly difficult to escape, as portfolio returns must exceed the growing withdrawal percentage to prevent further portfolio depletion. Even if markets subsequently recover, the retirement portfolio cannot fully rebound because higher proportions of it have been withdrawn. Poor returns early in retirement can push the sustainable withdrawal rate well below what is implied by long-term average market returns. Retirees experience heightened vulnerability to sequence-of-return risk when they begin spending from their investment portfolios. What happens in the markets during the fragile decade around the retirement date matters a lot.

Finally, spending shocks are surprise expenses beyond the planned budget. Unexpected expenses come in many forms, including an unforeseen need to help family members, divorce, changes in tax laws or other public policy, home repairs, rising health-care and prescription costs, and long-term care. Retirees also face the risk that inflation will erode the purchasing power of their savings as they progress through retirement. Spending shocks require additional reserve assets to avoid having to spend assets intended to support the ongoing planned portion of the retirement budget.

For a planned retirement budget, the overall cost of retirement will be less with some combination of a shorter life, stronger market returns, and fewer spending shocks. But retirement could become quite expensive when a long life is combined with poor market returns and significant spending shocks. The danger is that a combination of risks contributes to an overall retirement cost that exceeds available assets. An important theme for this book is to demonstrate how a reverse mortgage may assist in managing these risks.

2. *Play the long game.* To manage longevity risk, you should base your retirement income strategy on planning to live, not planning to die. A long life will be expensive to support, and it should take precedence. Fight the impatience that could lead you to choose short-term expediencies that carry greater long-term costs. This does not mean, however, that you must sacrifice short-term satisfactions to plan for the long term. Many efficiencies can be gained from a long-term focus that can sustain a higher living standard.

You must still plan for a long life, even when rejecting strategies that only help in the event of a long life. Remember, planning for average life expectancy is quite risky—by definition, half of the population outlives it. Planning to live longer means spending less than otherwise. Developing a plan that incorporates efficiencies that will not be realized until later can allow more spending today in anticipation of those efficiencies. Not taking such long-term, efficiency-improving actions will lead to a permanently reduced standard of living.

Some examples of focusing on the long-term plan over accepting short-term expediencies include:

- delaying the start of Social Security benefits,
- purchasing income annuities,
- paying taxes today to enjoy more substantial tax reductions in the future,
- planning to better support the ability to age in place,
- planning for the risk of cognitive decline at advanced age,
- developing an estate plan, and
- opening a line of credit with a reverse mortgage.

These strategies may not make much sense if the planning horizon is only a couple of years, but they may make a great deal of sense for someone building a sustainable long-term retirement income plan.

3. *Do not leave money on the table.* The holy grail of retirement income planning is a set of strategies that enhance retirement efficiency. I define efficiency this way: If one strategy simultaneously allows for the same or more lifetime spending alongside a greater legacy value for assets, relative to another strategy, then it is more efficient. Efficiency must be defined from

the perspective of how long you live. This underscores how I explain different reverse mortgage strategies in the book: Strategies that can better support a spending goal while also leaving a larger net legacy for heirs are simply more efficient and preferable from my point of view.

4. *Use reasonable expectations for portfolio returns.* A key lesson for long-term financial planning is that you should not expect to earn the average historical market returns for your portfolio. Half of the time realized returns will be less. Dismiss any retirement projection based on 8 percent or 12 percent returns, as the reality is likely much less when we account for portfolio volatility, inflation, and a desire to develop a plan that will work more than half the time.

5. *Be careful about plans that only work with high market returns.* A natural mathematical formula that applies to retirement planning is that higher assumed future market returns imply higher sustainable spending rates. Bonds provide a fixed rate of return when held to maturity, and stocks potentially offer a higher return than bonds as a reward for the additional risk. But a "risk premium" is not guaranteed. Retirees who spend more today because they are planning for higher market returns are essentially "amortizing their upside." They are spending more today than justified by bond investments, based on an assumption that higher returns in the future will make up the difference and justify the higher spending rate.

For retirees, the fundamental nature of risk is the threat that poor market returns trigger a permanently lower standard of living. Retirees must decide how much risk to their lifestyle they are willing to accept. Assuming that a risk premium on stocks will be earned, and therefore spending more today, is risky behavior. It may be reasonable behavior for the more risk tolerant among us, but it is not an appropriate behavior for everyone. It is important to think through the consequences in advance.

6. *Build an integrated strategy to manage various retirement risks.* A good retirement income strategy combines the best retirement income tools for meeting one's goals while protecting against longevity risk, market volatility and macroeconomic risks, and inflation and spending shocks. Manage these risks by combining income tools with different relative strengths and weaknesses for each of them.

7. *Approach retirement income tools with an agnostic view.* The financial-services profession generally divides into two camps: one on investment solutions and the other on insurance solutions. Both sides have adherents who see little use for the other side. But both sides have a role to play based on the preferences and concerns of individual retirees. It is potentially harmful to dismiss subsets of retirement income tools without a thorough investigation of their purported roles. Most relevant for this book is to avoid dismissing reverse mortgages without further consideration.

8. *Start by assessing all household assets and liabilities.* The retirement balance sheet is the starting point for building a retirement income strategy.

The first step involves quantifying retirement financial goals. These goals define the retirement expenses, or liabilities, to be funded. Financial goals include maximizing spending power (lifestyle) in such a way that spending can remain consistent and sustainable without any drastic reductions, no matter how long the retirement lasts (longevity). Other important goals may include leaving assets for subsequent generations (legacy) and maintaining sufficient reserves for unplanned contingencies (liquidity). Lifestyle, longevity, legacy, and liquidity are the four L's of retirement income. Effort is needed to figure out a realistic retirement budget, as well as placing a monetary value on legacy goals and reserves for contingencies.

A retirement plan involves more than just financial assets. Assets should be matched to liabilities with comparable levels of risk. Many assets can be used as part of the retirement income plan, and they can be generalized as reliable income assets, diversified portfolios, and reserves. Assets include investment accounts, retirement accounts, future work, Social Security benefits, home equity, life insurance and other insurance policies, and even family or community support. Depending on the strategy chosen, a reverse mortgage can allow home equity to be treated as reliable income ("tenure payment"), diversified portfolio (coordination strategy), or as reserves (preserve the growing line of credit to manage spending shocks).

Exhibit 1.2
Retirement Income Optimization Map©

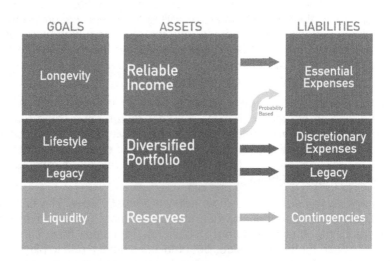

Next is the process of matching assets to liabilities. This can be done either on a balance-sheet level, using the present values of asset and liability streams, or on a period-by-period basis to match assets to ongoing spending needs. Structuring the retirement-income problem in this way makes it easier to keep track of the different aspects of the plan and to make sure that each liability has a funding source. This also allows retirees to more easily determine whether they have sufficient assets to meet their retirement needs or if they may be underfunded.

This organizational framework also serves as a foundation for deciding on an appropriate asset allocation and for seeing clearly how different retirement income tools fit into an overall plan. It also pushes us to think beyond just the investment portfolio and to contemplate how substantial assets like home equity can best serve an overall plan. Exhibit 1.2 provides a basic overview of this asset and liability mapping.

The Intuition for Reverse Mortgages

Understanding how reverse mortgages can add value in retirement planning requires an understanding about the peculiarities of sequence-of-return risk that the reverse mortgage can help to manage. When combined with a long retirement, sequence-of-return risk can lead to some potentially unanticipated outcomes regarding what types of strategies may work to support retirement sustainability. Sequence-of-return risk is a fascinating concept in that minor spending tweaks can have major implications for portfolio sustainability by impacting the amount of investment wealth that remains at the end of the planning horizon. This is the intuition I hope to help you develop in this section, as this will be key to recognizing why the later analysis of reverse mortgages in Chapters 5 to 8 works and is not "too good to be true."

We proceed by examining these peculiarities using an example from the historical data that will serve as a baseline for comparing different reverse mortgage strategies later in the book. In the case study detailed further in Chapter 5, a 62-year-old recently retired couple is working to create a retirement plan that will support their budget for 34 years through age 95. We will consider a simplified version of that case study in which the couple has $1 million of investment assets in a Roth IRA and is seeking to spend $39,485 per year plus inflation throughout their retirement with a balanced investment portfolio of 60 percent stocks and 40 percent bonds. This spending goal is chosen because it will cause their investment assets to deplete fully after covering their spending at age 95, using the market returns from 1962 to 1995.

Because the risk that a market downturn pushes the current withdrawal rate from remaining investments to an unsustainable level, the first sequence-risk synergy to note is that small changes to the initial withdrawal rate can have a large impact on portfolio sustainability. This situation is illustrated in Exhibit 1.3. With an initial withdrawal rate of 3.95 percent, the portfolio is depleted in 1995. The exhibit also shows portfolio sustainability for small withdrawal rate changes: 3.55 percent (-0.4 percent less), 3.75 percent (-0.2 percent less), 4.15 percent (0.2 percent more), and 4.35 percent (0.4 percent more).

While 3.95 percent as a withdrawal rate left $0 at the end of 1995, with a 3.55 percent withdrawal rate there is still $2.07 million remaining in 1995 dollars. With a smaller withdrawal rate reduction to 3.75 percent, remaining wealth at the end of 1995 would have been $1.03 million. In nominal terms, initial retirement wealth has been left intact. Meanwhile, had the withdrawal rate been just 0.2 percent higher, the portfolio would have depleted four years sooner, in 1992, after covering about a quarter of the spending. Meanwhile, a 4.35 percent withdrawal rate would have led the funds to run out in 1989, or about 6.5 years earlier than otherwise.

Exhibit 1.3
Sequence Risk and the Impact of Changing the Initial Withdrawal Rate

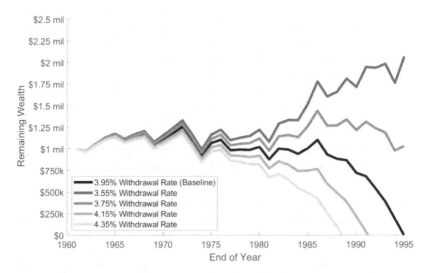

The key lesson is that the peculiarities of sequence-of-return risk cause small changes to the initial distribution rate to have a large impact on portfolio sustainability. An investment portfolio can be better preserved through minor reductions in the distributions taken from it. This does not have to mean spending less in retirement, as a lower portfolio withdrawal rate can be offset by spending from other assets. We will demonstrate how a reverse mortgage can play this role in reducing pressures on the investment portfolio. Possibilities include using tenure payments to cover part of the spending need, refinancing a traditional mortgage into a reverse mortgage to remove this fixed expense from the early retirement years, purchasing a home in part with a reverse mortgage, and using a reverse mortgage to help fund the delay of Social Security benefits.

A second approach to managing sequence risk is to have other assets held outside the investment portfolio to draw from as a temporary resource when the portfolio looks to be in trouble. Returns on these assets should not be correlated with the financial portfolio, since the purpose of these outside assets is to support spending when the portfolio is at greater risk.

To better understand the potential synergies created by a "buffer" asset, Exhibit 1.4 highlights how skipping single years of portfolio distributions can dramatically impact the final portfolio balance. The idea is that the external buffer asset provides a resource to cover any skipped distributions from the portfolio, leaving the portfolio in a much better position to rebound. This is based on the same example as previously described, with a 3.95 percent initial withdrawal rate causing the $1 million portfolio to deplete in 1995 if all 34 distributions are taken, with a retirement based on market returns starting in 1962. With these historical returns, the investment portfolio lost 7.4 percent in 1969, 8.6 percent in 1973, and 11.1 percent in 1974. If the retiree skipped taking the distribution in only 1970, which is the year after the 1969 market drop, and took the other 33 distributions, there would still be $710,197 left to spend at the end of 1995. By skipping the distribution only in 1974, after the 1973 drop, there would still be $687,922 at the end of 1995. If this couple instead skipped the 1975 distribution, reflecting the year after the 1974 drop, then $865,116 would remain in 1995. Going further with this, if the couple skipped all three of these distributions, they would wind up with $2.26 million remaining in 1995 instead of $0. These are big differences, but they are not even as big as could be shown with other historical examples, as the sequence risk impact on these years is relatively mild. The first notable market drop did not happen until the 8th year of retirement.

Exhibit 1.4
Sequence Risk and the Portfolio Impact of Skipping a Year of Distributions

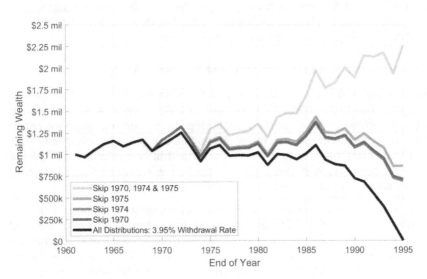

Nevertheless, skipping one distribution helped keep the portfolio on course and avoided the ongoing distribution rate from accelerating to unsustainable levels as remaining portfolio wealth declines. This sequence risk synergy provides a second means for understanding how a reverse mortgage could help to support retirement spending. Instead of just skipping the distributions for these years, the couple could source them from a line of credit on a reverse mortgage. This provides a sophisticated technique to grapple with sequence-of-return risk by only spending from the reverse mortgage when the retiree is vulnerable to locking in portfolio losses. The portfolio coordination strategies described in Chapter 5 will show how to treat the reverse mortgage line of credit as a buffer asset to help protect the investment portfolio from sequence risk.

The reverse mortgage creates costs in terms of initial setup costs and the ongoing loan balance growth for the borrowed amount, but the intuition shown here helps to explain how the reverse mortgage can contribute significant value by helping to manage sequence risk and preserve the investment portfolio, such that the benefits are able to exceed the costs.

In isolation, a reverse mortgage can look expensive. But it should not be viewed in isolation. It is a piece of a larger puzzle that retirees are trying to solve. Reverse mortgage costs can be offset by gains elsewhere in the overall financial plan through the ability to help manage sequence-of-return risk. With the example in Exhibit 1.4, for instance, if the loan balance for a reverse mortgage used to fund the retirement spending in 1970, 1974, and 1975 is less than $2.26 million, then beneficiaries can pay the loan balance and still have more left over in their investments to support a larger overall legacy. This is the type of scenario we will put to the test in later chapters. The punchline: Strategic reverse mortgage use can work to protect the investment portfolio from incurring excessive distributions by helping to manage the erratic behavior caused by a market downturn on a retirement spending plan funded through a volatile investment portfolio.

Understanding Your Retirement Income Style

Soon we will get into the specifics of housing wealth and decisions in retirement. But first, I think it's important to have a general sense of what retirement entails. An important first step in retirement planning is to determine your retirement income style, as this will guide how you may think about numerous other issues and decisions that are part of your overall retirement plan. As a preview for the book, I will also comment on how different retirement styles relate to potential reverse mortgage uses.

If you have spent much time reading about retirement income, it quickly becomes apparent that there are vastly different viewpoints about the best way to approach retirement spending. Some people love the stock market; others hate it. Some love annuities; others hate them. The same goes for life insurance, reverse mortgages, long-term-care insurance, and various other products and tools. Commentators argue about questions such as whether there is such a thing as a safe withdrawal rate from an investment portfolio, whether annuities provide enough value for their costs, and whether it is better to start Social Security as soon as possible or to defer collecting benefits until age 70.

The financial services profession remains quite siloed. There is an old saying that if the only tool you have is a hammer, then everything starts to look like a nail. This tendency is alive and well as those on the investment side tend to view an investment portfolio as the solution for any problem, while those on the insurance side tend to view insurance products as the answer for any financial question. Financial advisors and other pundits tend to support the approach they feel most comfortable with or are otherwise licensed or incentivized to provide, with little consideration for what may be best for any given individual. The prevalent idea is that there is one objectively superior retirement income approach for everyone, and anyone suggesting otherwise must be guided by a conflict of interest.

The reality is that there are competing viable approaches for retirement income. No one approach or retirement income product works best for everyone. Understanding which approach is best for you requires knowing more about your preferences and style. This can also save time and money, as adopting a strategy that fails to align with your preferences can lead to a plan that is poorly implemented throughout retirement. You need to be comfortable with your strategy and choose it for reasons other than because you have heard that it was the best way to do things.

With having long held the "Professor of Retirement Income" academic job title, I have felt it to be my responsibility to understand the different strategies that exist around creating a retirement income plan. In 2012, I attempted to outline the characteristics of two fundamentally different philosophies for retirement income planning—which I called probability-based and safety-first. I still remember working on this during the subway rides back and forth to the university in Tokyo, where I taught at that time. These philosophies diverge on the critical issue of where a retirement plan is best served: in the risk/reward trade-offs of a diversified and aggressive investment portfolio, or in the contractual protections of insurance products to fund essential spending needs before turning to investments to cover the rest.

Strong disagreements exist about how to position a retiree's assets to best meet retirement goals. The guidance and strategies provided to retirees still largely depend on the viewpoints of the pundit, whether that person works in the media, the financial services profession, or as a personal finance blogger. What is missing is the concept that there are multiple appropriate ways to approach retirement. Each pundit will have a personal style that may be different from the style of the individual receiving that message, which creates misalignment. Individuals optimize for different outcomes based on personal styles. They have characteristics that can be determined to better position a strategy that is right for them, rather than hoping for an alignment achieved through random matching with the viewpoint that's telling them what is "objectively right."

When I described distinctions between probability-based and safety-first, they were based on observations about how different commentators in the retirement income space described optimal retirement approaches. We now understand that these distinctions can be attributed to real and observable preferences.

Alex Murguia and I developed a survey that tested and quantified the role of six specific and distinct retirement income factors that make up a retirement income style. These factors identify a range of preferences around retirement finances. It is amazing how well they work together to define styles that directly translate into a taxonomy of specific retirement income strategies. These factors may also be helpful in thinking about whether reverse mortgages have a role in your plan.

We were able to formally demonstrate the importance of two main sets of factors and four supporting factors. The two main factors that can best capture an individual's retirement income style are Probability-Based vs. Safety-First and Optionality vs. Commitment Orientation. The other four factors play a secondary role through their correlations with the primary factors to help further identify retirement income strategies. These are a Time-Based vs. Perpetuity income floor, Accumulation vs. Distribution, Front-Loading vs. Back-Loading income, and True vs. Technical Liquidity. As this is meant as an introduction, I will just describe the two primary factors here.

With the first factor, we use the probability-based and safety-first names. The *Probability-Based vs. Safety-First* factor details how individuals prefer to source their retirement income from assets. Probability-based income sources are dependent on the potential for market growth to continuously provide a sustainable retirement income stream. This includes a traditional diversified investment portfolio or other assets that have the expectation of growth with realized capital gains supporting retirement income. Meanwhile, Safety-First income incorporates contractual obligations. The spending provided through these sources is less exposed to market swings. A safety-first approach may include protected sources of income common with defined-benefit pensions, annuities with lifetime income protections, and individual government bonds held to maturity. The safety-first approach does not depend on an expectation of market growth to provide capital gains as a source of spending, since the income is contractually driven. Though no strategy is completely safe, the inclusion of contractual protections implies a relative degree of safety compared to relying on unknown market outcomes.

The second main factor reflects the dimension of preferences for *Optionality vs. Commitment*. This approach details the degree of flexibility sought with income strategies. Optionality reflects a preference for keeping options open for retirement income. Those with an optionality preference want to maintain flexibility with their strategies to respond to more favorable economic developments or to a changing personal situation. This preference aligns with retirement solutions that do not have predetermined holding periods and are amenable to making changes.

Conversely, commitment reflects a preference for committing to a retirement income solution. There is less concern with potentially unfavorable economic developments or a worsening personal situation because the solution solves for a lifetime retirement income need. The security of having a dedicated retirement income solution outweighs missing out on potentially more positive future outcomes, and it may provide further satisfaction from having made decisions and not feeling a lingering sensation that this retirement income decision-making process must remain on your to-do list. Planning to manage potential cognitive decline and to protect family members who may not be as financially savvy can also be a source of satisfaction in this approach.

Your scores on these factors help to identify retirement income styles that will map to specific retirement income strategies that may resonate with you as a starting point for your retirement. To explain this, Alex and I created the Retirement Income Style Awareness® (RISA®) Profiles, based on the RISA Matrix® shown in Exhibit 1.5. The RISA Profile® is effectively a replacement for measuring risk tolerance that is broader and includes more dimensions to be better suited to the complexities of retirement income planning. The RISA Matrix lays out how the scores calculated for each RISA factor can be utilized and matched to appropriate retirement income strategies.

Exhibit 1.5
The RISA Matrix

This process relies on the idea that even though these six factors are statistically distinct from one another and reflect unique characteristics, there are some correlations found between them. As those correlations work together, we can identify retirement income styles and strategies that match.

I noted that the statistical analysis identified the two main factors as probability-based vs. safety-first and commitment vs. optionality. We created the RISA Matrix to show the intersection of these preferences. The scale for probability-based vs. safety-first is aligned horizontally, and optionality vs. commitment is aligned vertically. This creates four distinct retirement income strategy quadrants, each of which is based on an individual's scores for these two main RISA factors. Important to this as well is that the probability-based perspective is correlated with a preference for optionality, while those with a safety-first outlook tend to be more commitment oriented. The four supporting factors are mixed in, too, through their correlations with the main factors, to identify strategies more strongly.

From the available retirement income strategies, we identify four main classes to match the four quadrants within the RISA Matrix. These are total return, risk wrap, income protection, and time segmentation (or bucketing). These strategies align closely with the common framework of systematic withdrawals (total return), time segmentation, and essential vs. discretionary (income protection and risk wrap). Although I am introducing these approaches now, I do have other volumes in the *Retirement Researcher's Guide Series* that explore these various strategies in greater depth.

Total-Return Investing

Starting at the upper-right quadrant of the RISA Matrix, these are individuals whose preferences lean toward both probability-based and optionality. Typically, individuals with these characteristics identify with drawing income from a diversified investment portfolio rather than using contractual sources to fund their retirement expenses. Investors rely on portfolio growth to support their spending and do not want to commit to a strategy. Those who value optionality wish to maintain the ability to consider retirement income withdrawal options. Drawing from secondary characteristics, they are also more comfortable with seeking market growth despite the volatility it can create. The individual is likely to prefer a more variable income stream with the potential for investment growth rather than a stable retirement income stream with more muted potential growth. They want to enjoy their early retirement years and are willing to accept the risk that they may have to make spending cuts later.

This quadrant provides the combination of preferences that I have written about in the past as probability-based. These are investment-centric approaches that rely on earning the risk premium from the stock market. Stocks are expected to outperform bonds over sufficiently long periods, and this investment outperformance will provide retirees with the opportunity to fund a better lifestyle. Should decent market returns materialize and sufficiently outpace inflation, investment solutions can be sustained indefinitely to support retirement goals. Those favoring investments rely on the notion that while the stock market is volatile, it will eventually provide favorable returns and will outperform bonds. The upside potential from an investment portfolio is viewed as so significant that insurance products are not needed. Investment approaches are probability-based in the sense that they will *probably* work.

This retirement income strategy originated from research conducted by California-based financial planner William Bengen in the 1990s. Bengen sought to determine the safe withdrawal rate from a financial portfolio over a long retirement. Though the term *safe withdrawal rate* uses the word "safe," it is not part of the safety-first approach. The probability-based school uses "safe" in a historical context as based on what could have worked when tested with historical market returns. The question is: How much can retirees withdraw from their savings, which are invested in a diversified portfolio, while still maintaining sufficient confidence that they can safely continue spending without running out of wealth?

Finding strategies that could have always worked with historical data make probability-based advocates feel comfortable. Probability-based advocates are generally more optimistic about the long-run potential of stocks to outperform bonds, so retirees are generally advised to take on as much risk as they can tolerate to minimize the probability of plan failure. Answers about asset allocation for retirees generally point to holding around 40 percent to 80 percent of the retirement portfolio in stocks. The individuals whose style places them in this quadrant are more likely to subscribe to a systematic withdrawal strategy for retirement income, based on a total return investing approach.

Those with a total-return style are comfortable with the stock market and seek to further leverage their investment portfolios for long-term growth. Potential reverse mortgage uses that will serve this role include refinancing an existing mortgage instead of carrying it into retirement, building a bridge to help support delaying Social Security, and using the "HECM for Purchase" as part of purchasing a new home in retirement.

Income Protection

The lower-left quadrant is home to individuals with a safety-first and commitment orientation. These characteristics align with retirement income strategies traditionally referred to as essential vs. discretionary or income flooring. Assets are positioned to match the risk characteristics of a spending goal. There is a preference for contractually protected lifetime income to cover essential retirement expenses, while a more diversified total return portfolio is used only for discretionary expenses. These characteristics associate with using income annuities to provide greater spending protection with a lifetime commitment.

This quadrant reflects the set of characteristics that I have described over my years of writing about retirement income as safety-first. Safety-first advocates are generally more willing to accept a role for insurance as a source of income protection to help manage various retirement risks. For investment-only strategies, retirement risks are generally managed by spending less in retirement, as longevity risk is managed by assuming a long life and market risk is managed by assuming poor market returns. But insurance companies can pool these market and longevity risks across a large base of retirees—much like traditional defined-benefit pensions and Social Security—allowing for retirement spending that is more closely aligned with average long-term fixed-income returns and average longevity. Those with average lengths of life and average market returns will have paid an insurance premium that is transferred to those who experience a more costly combination of a longer retirement and poor market returns. This could support a better lifestyle than what is feasible for someone self-managing these risks and who is more nervous about the possibility of relying on market growth to avoid outliving assets.

Those more comfortable with the safety-first approach believe that contractual guarantees are reliable and that staking their retirement income on the assumption that favorable market returns will eventually arrive is emotionally overwhelming and dangerous. These individuals are more concerned about market risk, as a retiree gets only one opportunity for a successful retirement. Essential spending needs, at least, should not be subject to market whims. The safety-first school views investment-only solutions as undesirable because the retiree retains all the longevity and market risks, which an insurance company is better positioned to manage. Contractual-based and committed income strategies that do not rely on market growth are viewed as appropriate for core retirement expenses.

With an income protection style, a big emphasis can be placed on using the tenure payment option from a reverse mortgage as a source of reliable income covered through home equity. Those with an income protection style may also be attracted to refinancing a traditional mortgage to reduce cash flow needs in early retirement, or creating a Social Security delay bridge with the emphasis on maximizing protected income through Social Security.

Risk Wrap

The remaining two quadrants reflect hybrid styles that can better align with the preferences of retirees who may not hold all the natural correlations between different retirement income factors. Shifting to the lower-right quadrant of the RISA Matrix, we find individuals whose RISA Profile shows both probability-based and commitment orientations.

While individuals here maintain a probability-based outlook with a desire for market participation, they also have desire to commit to a solution that provides a structured income stream. Income annuities, which require an irreversible commitment and a lack of growth potential, tend to be nonstarters for these individuals. These individuals wish to seek growth, but they also worry more about outliving their assets and are more comfortable with committing to strategies. For these reasons, using only unprotected investment portfolios is not attractive.

Since the 1990s, the retirement industry has been creating structured tools that are more aligned with the combinations of preferences found in this quadrant. We use the term "risk wrap" as a general description of such tools. A risk wrap strategy provides a blend of investment growth opportunities with lifetime income benefits, generally through a variable or indexed annuity. Such tools can be designed to offer upside growth potential alongside secured lifetime spending even if markets perform poorly.

Those with a risk wrap style may also appreciate using the tenure payment option as a source of reliable income, as well as portfolio coordination strategies that use the reverse mortgage as a buffer asset to help manage market volatility in retirement.

Time Segmentation

Finally, the upper-left quadrant identifies another hybrid case. These are individuals with both safety-first and optionality preferences. They like contractual protections, but they also prefer optionality.

Those whose factor scores place them in this quadrant reflect a desire for retirement income solutions that are characterized by contractually driven income while still maintaining a high level of flexibility to change strategies or accommodate ongoing changes. It can be difficult to enter a contract while keeping options open, but the retirement world has addressed this challenge with strategies related to investment-based bucketing or time segmentation. While annuities with lifetime commitments are less likely to appeal to individuals in this quadrant, these retirees may be satisfied with holding individual bonds to cover upcoming expenses.

A time-segmentation or bucketing strategy usually sources short-term retirement income needs with a rolling bond ladder or other fixed income assets. Bond ladders are frequently implemented with contractually protected instruments (cash equivalents or government-issued securities) that can be used for shorter to intermediate income needs, with a diversified investment portfolio designed for longer-term expenses. That growth portfolio will be used to gradually replenish the short-term buckets as those assets are used to cover retirement expenses. It also provides the desired optionality.

There is much debate about whether these strategies are materially different from using total-return investing. In terms of behavior, these strategies do have an important difference from a total-return portfolio if they help people who have this style's characteristics to be more comfortable with a growth portfolio. Short-term spending protections could help some retirees get through bouts of market volatility without panicking. That behavioral aspect is primarily where the value can lie. Much like risk wrap strategies, time segmentation reflects a hybrid approach that can match a less natural combination of preferences held by these retirees and therefore satisfy a behavioral need.

Those with a time segmentation style might look to the term payment option from a reverse mortgage to construct a bucket for short-term spending needs, or they may look to have a growing line of credit as an optional source of contingency funds for unexpected expenses.

Discussions about retirement income planning can become quite confusing as there are so many different viewpoints expressed in the consumer media. Each individual investor must ultimately identify the style that can best support his or her financial and psychological needs for retirement. The RISA Profile provides a way for users to quickly identify the types of retirement strategies that may best align with their personal style.

Invitation to Identify Your Retirement Income Style

If you would like further guidance, we have created the RISA Profile questionnaire to help you quickly find your retirement style.

I would like to offer you, as a reader, the opportunity to take this questionnaire and receive a free RISA Profile report. This will let you know where your preferences align in terms of the four quadrants of the RISA Matrix. Knowing your RISA Profile may provide more context for thinking through different possible uses for a reverse mortgage, among other matters.

To do this, please visit **www.risaprofile.com/reverse** to take the questionnaire and obtain your RISA Profile results without cost or any further obligation. And please feel free to share your feedback with me as this is a new tool we are constantly striving to improve (**wade@retirementresearcher.com**).

Potential Strategies for a HECM Reverse Mortgage

The next few chapters discuss important preliminaries. Chapter 2 is about general housing decisions for retirement and important concepts around aging in place. Chapter 3 discusses the background and history of reverse mortgages in the United States. Chapter 4 describes how reverse mortgages work. Chapters 5 to 8 provide the heart of the book. Conventional wisdom treats the home as a reserve asset that will not be touched, other than to serve as a last resort option to meet spending and long-term-care needs once other assets are depleted. Otherwise, it becomes a source of legacy. These chapters provide quantitative assessments to compare this conventional wisdom against other reverse mortgage strategies for a fuller view of the reverse mortgage's role in a responsible plan.

It is worth stepping back to summarize the retirement income problem we seek to solve, which has been the focus of this chapter. Retirees must support a series of expenses—overall lifestyle spending goals, unexpected contingencies, legacy goals—to enjoy a successful retirement. Suppose that retirees only have two assets—beyond Social Security and pensions—to meet their spending obligations: an investment portfolio and home equity. The task is to link these assets to spending obligations efficiently while also mitigating retirement risks such as longevity, market volatility and the sequence of returns, and spending surprises.

The fundamental question is this: How can investments and home equity work together to meet spending goals while simultaneously preserving remaining assets to cover contingencies and support a legacy? Spending from either asset today means less for future spending and legacy. For the portfolio, spending reduces the remaining asset balance and sacrifices subsequent growth on those investments. Likewise, spending a portion of home equity surrenders future legacy. Both effects work in the same way, so the question is how to best coordinate the use of these two assets to meet the spending goals and still preserve as much legacy as possible.

When a household has an investment portfolio and home equity, the "default" strategy tends to value spending down investment assets first and preserving home equity, with the goal of supporting a legacy through a debt-free home. A reverse mortgage is viewed as a last resort once the investment portfolio has been depleted and vital spending needs are threatened.

As I will show, this conventional thinking is overly constraining and counterproductive. Initiating the reverse mortgage earlier and coordinating spending from home equity throughout retirement can help meet spending goals while also providing a larger legacy. This matches my definition of providing greater retirement income efficiency.

Legacy wealth is the combined value of any remaining financial assets plus any remaining home equity after repaying the reverse mortgage loan balance. Money is fungible, and the specific ratio of financial assets and remaining home equity is not important. In the final analysis, only the sum of these two components matters.

For heirs wishing to keep the home, a larger legacy offers an extra bonus of additional financial assets after the loan balance has been repaid. The home is *not* lost.

While taking money from the reverse mortgage reduces the home-equity component, it does not necessarily reduce the overall net worth or legacy value of assets. Wanting to specifically preserve the home may be a psychological constraint, which leads to a less efficient retirement. Should the heir wish to keep the house, the value of the house received as an inheritance can be redeployed for this purpose, with more leftover as well.

These chapters go into greater depth on the potential ways that a reverse mortgage can be used within a retirement income plan. Exhibit 1.6 provides a framework for organizing the potential strategies. Four general reverse mortgage utilization categories are: portfolio coordination for retirement spending (Chapter 5), debt coordination for housing (Chapter 6), as a resource to fund retirement income strategy enhancements (Chapter 7), and as "insurance" for various retirement contingencies (Chapter 8).

Exhibit 1.6
The Spectrum of Reverse Mortgage Strategies

Portfolio Coordination for Retirement Spending (Chapter 5)	Use HECM as a Last Resort
	Use Tenure Payments to Reduce Portfolio Withdrawals
	Coordinate HECM Spending to Mitigate Sequence Risk
Portfolio/Debt Coordination for Housing (Chapter 6)	Refinance Existing Mortgage to Eliminate Ongoing Payments
	HECM for Purchase for New Home
	Fund Home Renovations to Allow for Aging in Place
Funding Source for Retirement Efficiency Improvements (Chapter 7)	Social Security Delay Bridge
	Tax Bracket Management or Pay Taxes for Roth Conversions
	Tenure Payment as Annuity Alternative
	Pay Premiums for Existing Long-Term-Care Insurance Policy
Preserve Credit as Insurance Policy (Chapter 8)	Support Retirement Spending After Portfolio Depletion
	Protective Hedge for Home Value
	Provides Contingency Fund for Spending Shocks (In-home care, health expenses, divorce settlement)

Finally, Chapter 9 closes the book with practical advice about deciding on a reverse mortgage. This includes an assessment of reverse mortgage risks, along with tips on how to find a lender and other final thoughts.

Chapter 2: Housing Decisions in Retirement

Developing a plan to meet housing needs throughout retirement is important. Most retirees will continue to live at the same home as before retirement, but the thought of moving is a consideration for many and a reality for some. Some retirees will move multiple times throughout retirement. Housing options do multiply for retirees with greater flexibility to consider RV living, active adult communities, continuing care retirement communities, and living abroad, among other possibilities.

As part of this process, retirees should think about how housing needs may change during retirement in response to physical and cognitive decline. One or more moves may become necessary in retirement for health-related reasons, but planning can reduce both this need and its impact.

While a home provides an emotional anchor, shelter, memories, and proximity to friends and community, it is also a major source of wealth and a large fraction of net worth for retirees and near retirees. Using Survey of Consumer Finances data for 2019, the Urban Institute found that home equity represents 46 percent of overall net worth at the median for Americans age 65 to 74. Their median home value, which is not the same as home equity since many in this group still have outstanding mortgages, was $180,000, compared to having $104,000 of financial assets. For those age 75 and older, home equity rose to 55 percent of overall net worth. The median home value for this age group was $159,000, compared to $73,531 of financial assets.

In addition, expenses related to the home (property taxes, utility bills, home maintenance, and upkeep) can add up to a significant portion of the overall household budget. The Center for Retirement Research at Boston College analyzed numbers for retired couples age 65 to 74 and found that housing expenses represent 30 percent of the typical household budget.

In this chapter, we consider the characteristics for a good home in retirement and how can one support aging in place? These are key decisions in a retirement plan.

Do Retirees Move?

New retirees frequently feel more freedom and flexibility to live where they wish. While working and raising children, families are more firmly locked in place by proximity to employment and schools. Upon retirement, a move to a community with a less highly rated school and no daily commute could mean lower property taxes and increased savings for the retirement budget. There is the potential to improve finances by moving to a state with a more tax-friendly environment for retirees. This newfound freedom can create a whole new set of options.

Nevertheless, most retirees choose to stay put. Richard Green and Hyojung Lee studied households and found that the propensity to move peaks in an individual's 20s and then declines until about 50. Moving then stays at these lowest relative levels for higher ages. Older individuals are less likely to move, and the rate of moving does not rise at typical retirement ages. There is an uptick in moving at more advanced ages, but this reflects a need to move for health-related reasons or to receive institutional care.

In spring 2016, the American College of Financial Services conducted a survey of 1,003 people between the ages of 55 and 75 who had at least $100,000 of investment assets and $100,000 of home equity. When asked whether they planned to remain in their current home for as long as possible, 60 percent said yes, 23 percent said maybe, and 17 percent said no.

Similarly, a Merrill Lynch Retirement Study conducted in partnership with AgeWave showed that, among retirees age 50 and older, only 37 percent had moved in retirement while another 27 percent anticipated moving at some point and 36 percent had no plans to move. The most popular reason to not move was loving one's home, while important reasons for moving were listed as being closer to family, decreasing home expenses, fulfilling health needs, and changes in marital status.

The decision to move or stay put relates to priorities and preferences among numerous characteristics. We will return to topics relevant for those who choose to remain in the same home, but first we review relevant considerations for new retirees thinking about the best place to live.

Characteristics of a Good Place to Live in Retirement

Joseph Coughlin, the director of the MIT AgeLab, created three basic questions to identify quality-of-life issues for retirement:

- Who will change my lightbulbs?
- How will I get an ice cream cone?
- Whom will I have lunch with?

An essential part of answering these questions involves solving for the right type and location of housing. These questions illustrate how our lives will change as our bodies slow down and health issues or other aspects of aging make us less mobile.

For some early retirees, moving around frequently and traveling may be common, but these are important considerations for anyone considering settling down more permanently in one location.

These questions focus on whether we can continue to live in and properly maintain the same home, whether we have access to a community that lets us continue to enjoy basic conveniences even if we stop driving our own cars, and what will happen to our social lives and opportunities to remain active as old friends also become less mobile or move away.

Will we live in communities that keep these key aspects of quality living accessible to us? For new retirees, any difficulty answering these questions may still be in the distant future, but the major life changes associated with retirement provide a good opportunity to reflect on the different possibilities and develop a set of contingency plans.

Ultimately, one of the greatest dangers to quality of life in retirement is the risk of becoming increasingly isolated, with only television or web surfing to pass the time. On the emotional side, the housing decision may relate in large part to figuring out how to best answer Coughlin's three questions over the long term.

Because of its important connection to the emotional and financial aspects of retirement, it is worthwhile to think carefully about housing options and potential uses for home equity. The importance of living somewhere with social connections, transportation options, quality health care, and long-term-care services increases with age. In the more immediate present, you need to think about where to live, how long to stay there, and whether to move later in retirement. Plenty of justifications exist for staying put or for moving.

It is important to anticipate changing life needs in advance, since moving becomes more difficult as we age. Putting off these matters may result in the need to make quick and suboptimal decisions in the face of impairments that may arise. Planning around finding a good place to live and making the necessarily modifications in advance can allow for more desirable long-term outcomes.

Decisions to move must not be taken lightly. It is easy to make a move based on a vision that does not become reality. It is worth conducting a trial move by renting for a few months during different seasons to make sure that the move feels right. This way, if things do not work out as planned, you have avoided a potentially costly and difficult situation.

We consider reasons for moving, which can also relate to reasons for staying put if these priorities are already fulfilled. Issues relate primarily to the changing emphasis in life's priorities and needs. There are numerous considerations that each retiree will need to prioritize before deciding on the best option. The media provides rankings about the best places for retirees to live, which may involve different combinations of these factors. Such lists may be helpful, with ideas and important considerations, but the article's methodology may not match your priorities. Let us consider some of the important matters.

Affordability

First, affordability and retirement sustainability on the financial side are important. Housing is a major expense, and the current home may be larger and more expensive than necessary. Empty nesters may no longer require a home large enough to accommodate an entire family. Large homes require more cleaning, maneuvering, heating, cooling, and maintenance.

Many retirees will consider downsizing as one way to free up home equity for other retirement expenses. Downsizing does not necessarily mean moving to a physically smaller home; it can mean moving to a similar-sized home in a less expensive area. The arithmetic of converting home equity through downsizing is straightforward. If you pay off the mortgage on a $300,000 home, sell it, and move into a $200,000 home, you have freed up $100,000 of home equity for other uses. This may also reduce housing-related expenses.

An important caveat about downsizing is that it can be dangerous to assume that it will provide an important source of retirement funding. The same study of retirees conducted by Merrill Lynch and AgeWave also found what they refer to as a "downsize surprise," where many retirees who planned to downsize ended up not wanting to do so once they retired. For those who had moved since retirement, 51 percent moved to a smaller home, 19 percent to a same-size home, and 30 percent to a larger home. For those who chose to upsize, the most important reason given was to have more space for family members (including grandchildren) to visit. The AgeWave study makes clear that downsizing is not the only moving option for retirees, and it should not be viewed as a given.

Besides housing costs, one can also consider other cost-of-living expenses. How would the basic costs of daily living change in a new location? Are homeowner's insurance policies and utilities more expensive? Is it necessary to pay for trash pickup and other services? Consider as well that health insurance, health care, and long-term-care costs can vary dramatically by location.

Furthermore, what is the tax situation? Tax considerations include state income tax rates and whether some retirement income sources such as Social Security are excluded from state income taxes. State and local sales taxes, state inheritance taxes, and local property taxes are also important considerations to factor in the retirement budget when considering a move. With sales tax, one may also consider if certain categories of expenses, such as food or prescriptions, are exempt. There may also be local government programs to provide property-tax relief for senior citizens.

Home Ownership vs. Renting

Another consideration related to moving in retirement is simply selling your home and then renting a new place. This frees up home equity and provides the flexibility to make more frequent moves before settling down. Renting provides the option to change the living situation more frequently, and some retirees may value this and wish to move multiple times during retirement.

As for financial considerations, the home is a large, undiversified asset that may not appreciate over time. Many retirees will find themselves fortunate if their home value can maintain pace with inflation, though there are certainly opportunities for faster home appreciation in some parts of the country. By selling, home equity can be re-invested into a more diversified investment portfolio that may have the potential to earn higher long-term investment returns.

Also, though there will now be a rental expense, other retirement costs will reduce. First, property taxes are gone. Rent for an apartment may even be comparable to what was paid in property taxes on a family home in a good school district. There will be savings on home maintenance, repairs, and homeowner's insurance, too. Deciding whether to own or rent is an important consideration for retirees on the move.

Proximity to Family and Friends

Another important issue that becomes very personal is the location of family and friends. Does moving mean leaving such individuals behind? What are the odds of making friends in the new location? Alternatively, children may have moved to other parts of the country, and new retirees may wish to be closer to their grandchildren. If children and grandchildren live elsewhere, the tradeoffs may relate to remaining near friends or moving to be close to family. As today's new retirees are also called the sandwich generation, on account of their potential need to care for both their aging parents as well as their adult children or grandchildren, moves may also be related to these needs.

Maintaining social ties and not becoming isolated is important in retirement. Being close to family and friends can help in this regard. But meeting new people and developing a social network in a new community can fulfill this same purpose. It is important to have someone who can provide occasional checks and help you avoid isolation. As aging progresses, obtaining trusted support for lawn care, snow removal, home maintenance, cleaning, and food delivery can be very helpful. These are important considerations, especially for retirees who lack friends and family nearby to help with these matters.

Agreeable Climate, Community, & Leisure Activities

When considering a move, many opportunities exist for retirees to find communities with active networks for social activities related to specific hobbies or interests.

There are various living options for retirees during their more active years. Aside from continuing in the same home, opportunities include extensive traveling by RV or living abroad. They can involve communities organized by age, religion, lifestyle, recreational interests, or hobbies. Think, for example, of a neighborhood organized around a golf course. It could also be a college or university town that provides cultural opportunities and the ability to take courses or engage in other educational activities. Naturally occurring retirement communities are neighborhoods in which the residents gradually shifted toward being retirees over time and may work together to provide social support or other services for residents.

Active adult communities are another option. They are available both for ages 55+ (80 percent of residents must be at least 55) and 62+ (all residents must be at least 62). (These are the only housing options that allow age discrimination.) They can provide organized activities and social support. These types of communities generally do not provide health care or assisted-living options. But they are increasingly available in areas with favorable climates, in university towns, or in other places attractive to retirees.

When making a big move, it is important to consider the year-round climate. A place that was nice to visit in the winter may be unbearably hot in the summer. Tourist areas that may be lively during peak seasons can be dramatically different in the off-season. Especially when moving for reasons discussed here, a trial-run of renting in the area for an extended period can be valuable to ensure that it is the right fit. Concerns about the impact of climate change may also influence where to live.

Continuing-care retirement communities are another option that can provide social networking benefits as well as covering potential long-term-care needs. These can be an option for those seeking only to make one move and do not want to move again later for health reasons.

Opportunities for Part-Time Work

Anyone interested in working, part-time or full-time, or in volunteering, needs to consider whether a specific locale is conducive to these opportunities.

Health-Care and Long-Term-Care Options

Another consideration is the availability of high-quality medical facilities in the area. Those with specific health conditions may already understand the need to live close to specific medical facilities providing the needed care. For others, it is important to recognize that care needs may grow over time, so choosing a place located near first-class hospitals and medical facilities is an important part of aging in place.

When considering relocating, remember that Medicare Advantage and some other types of health insurance are location-specific for in-network care. Relocating may require changing Medicare options. Original Medicare may be a better choice for retirees who are frequently on the move.

Diverse Transportation Options

Finally, for long-term planners, it is important to consider the availability of transportation options outside of using your own car, such as public transportation, taxis or services like Uber, or volunteer services from non-profit organizations. Is the location walkable and accessible? An important part of planning involves less dependency on your own ability to drive a car. Being isolated in the suburbs could accelerate mental or emotional declines, and this can subsequently make a move more difficult. The aging process will slowly reduce mobility. Moving with long-term needs in mind will increase your chances of aging in place and maintaining quick access to important medical care.

Considerations for Settling More Permanently in a Home

Many retirees have family, community ties, and friendships that they do not wish to leave behind. Many have significant memories and good feelings about their homes and wish to maintain this stability and familiarity. A home can be an important part of one's emotional identity, so many people choose not to leave that anchor behind. Homeowners tend to take pride in ownership and might not care to go through the moving process again. New technologies and the possibility of renovating one's home can also make aging in place easier than in the past. After considering the points from the previous section, most retirees will decide that the best option is to remain in place in retirement. Others may move to a home where they anticipate remaining. We look now at some issues to help ensure that these options are sustainable.

Staying at home over the long-term requires anticipating future potential needs related to physical and cognitive limitations and making sure that life can continue comfortably at the same home. *Aging in place* refers to the growing industry around helping members of the aging population remain in their homes despite functional or cognitive impairments. New technologies and services are always coming on the market to support those wishing to age in place. By renovating an existing home, retirees can maintain familiarity and comfort, delaying or potentially avoiding any future move to institutional settings.

Merrill Lynch and AgeWave conducted a survey of retirees age 50 and older and found that 85 percent viewed their own home as the preferred location for receiving long-term care. Beyond this, 10 percent were looking at assisted living facilities, 4 percent considered moving in with other family members, and 1 percent expressed interest in nursing homes. Home care is often the more desirable and less expensive option, and it can be extended with sufficient planning. In addition, government agencies have expressed support for the idea and have promoted the concept, as aging in place often requires less contribution from government programs such as Medicaid than nursing homes or assisted-living facilities do.

Professionals can provide guidance about specific home renovations to better support aging in place. Universal design features and other characteristics that can lay a stronger foundation for aging in place include:

- Walk-in showers, grab bars, and other bathroom safety features;
- Single-floor living with no stairs (kitchen, bathing facility, and bedroom are all on one floor), or an elevator allowing access to other floors;
- Wheelchair accessibility: ramps to the home, wide doors and hallways that can accommodate a wheelchair, and at least one wheelchair-accessible entrance to the home;
- Levers for door handles and faucets rather than twisting knobs;
- Good lighting in case sight is diminished;
- Accessible cabinets and closets as well as lowered counters to allow for cooking while sitting;
- Softened non-skid flooring to help cushion any falls, but no rugs or other floor items that could create a tripping hazard;
- Electric controls and switches that can be reached while sitting;
- New technologies to monitor health status and medicine use.

The planning required to age in place offers several potential paths depending on your specific desires and needs. If you stay put, renovating your home can make it livable even if you have physical or cognitive impairments. If you move, you can look for a new home with the necessary renovations already in place and a community where many types of care are readily accessible. By ensuring that these steps are taken, you can avoid future health-related moves, which is an important goal for most retirees. The further reading section also provides a link to the *AARP HomeFit Guide* that offers more ideas about how to improve the comfort and safety of your home.

Chapter 3: Background and History of Reverse Mortgages

If, after considering other housing options, you have decided to remain in an eligible home (or are moving into one), you may want to consider a Home Equity Conversion Mortgage (HECM – commonly pronounced "heck-um")—more commonly known as a "reverse mortgage."

The vast majority of reverse mortgages in the United States are HECM reverse mortgages, which are regulated and insured through the federal government by the Department of Housing and Urban Development (HUD) and the Federal Housing Authority (FHA). Other proprietary options exist outside of the federal program, which we will review in Chapter 4.

The HECM program includes both fixed- and variable-rate loans. Fixed-rate loans only allow proceeds to be taken as an initial lump sum, with no subsequent access to a line of credit. They are also not commonly used. Two cases where a fixed-rate HECM might be a relevant consideration include when the strategy is to refinance a large existing mortgage or when using the HECM for Purchase program. Otherwise, this book is primarily focused on variable-rate HECM options that allow for the line of credit. Variable-rate HECMs are also known as adjustable-rate HECMs.

In the past, any discussion of reverse mortgages as a retirement income tool typically focused on real or perceived negatives related to traditionally high costs and potentially inappropriate uses of funds. These conversations often included misguided ideas about the homeowner losing title to the home and hyperbole about the "American Dream" becoming the "American Nightmare." Reverse mortgages have been portrayed as a desperate last resort.

However, developments over the past decade have made reverse mortgages harder to dismiss outright. he federal government has been refining regulations for its HECM program to:

- improve the mortgage insurance fund's sustainability,
- better protect eligible nonborrowing spouses, and
- ensure that borrowers have sufficient financial resources to continue paying their property taxes, homeowner's insurance, and home-maintenance expenses.

The thrust of these changes has been to ensure that reverse mortgages are used responsibly, as part of an overall retirement income strategy.

On the academic side, a growing body of research has demonstrated how responsible use of a reverse mortgage can enhance an overall retirement income plan. Importantly, this research incorporates realistic costs for reverse mortgages, both in relation to their initial upfront costs and the ongoing growth of any outstanding loan balance. Quantified benefits are understood to exist only after netting out the costs associated with reverse mortgages.

Well-handled reverse mortgages have suffered too long from bad press surrounding irresponsible use. Reverse mortgages give responsible retirees the option to create liquidity for an otherwise illiquid asset, which can, in turn, potentially support a more efficient retirement income strategy (more spending and/or more legacy). Liquidity is created by allowing homeowners to borrow against the value of the home with the flexibility to defer repayment until they have permanently left the home. This makes it possible to use housing wealth as part of a coordinated spending plan for retirement.

The media has been picking up on these developments, and coverage about reverse mortgages is much more positive today. But this trend of positive coverage is still a new phenomenon, and with so much preexisting bias, it can be hard to view reverse mortgages objectively without a clear understanding of how the benefits may exceed the costs.

How Reverse Mortgages Can Help a Retirement Plan

Two benefits give opening a reverse mortgage early in retirement the potential to improve retirement efficiencies despite loan costs. First, coordinating withdrawals from a reverse mortgage reduces strain on portfolio withdrawals, which helps manage sequence-of-return risk. Investment volatility is amplified by sequence-of-return risk and can be more harmful to retirees who are withdrawing from, rather than contributing to, their portfolios. Reverse mortgages sidestep this sequence risk by providing an alternative source of spending that reduces pressure on making portfolio distributions.

The second potential benefit of opening the reverse mortgage early is that the principal limit that can be borrowed from will continue to grow throughout retirement. Reverse mortgages are non-recourse loans, meaning that even if the loan balance is greater than the subsequent home value, the borrowers or their beneficiaries/estate do not have to repay more than what the home is worth. Sufficiently long retirements carry a reasonable possibility that the available credit may eventually exceed the value of the home. In these cases, mortgage insurance premiums paid to the government are used to make sure that the lender does not experience a loss. This line-of-credit growth is one of the most important and confusing aspects of reverse mortgages. I will return to line-of-credit growth later.

As the government continues to strengthen the rules and regulations for reverse mortgages, and new research continues to pave the way with an agnostic view of their role, reverse mortgages may become much more common in the coming years.

As gerontologist Dr. Sandra Timmerman has said:

> The transition to retirement is a wake-up call for many middle-income Baby Boomers who haven't saved enough money to last a lifetime and want to age in place. With their homes as a major untapped financial resource, the smart use of reverse mortgages will be their saving grace.

Addressing the Bad Reputation of Reverse Mortgages

Before moving too far in discussing how reverse mortgages can fit into a retirement income plan, it is worthwhile to consider further how their bad reputation initially developed. Some aspects were based on misunderstandings, such as the idea that the lender receives the title to the home, or simple miscommunication among family members about future inheritances. Other troubles relate to problems that have since been corrected by new HUD regulations, such as concerns about withdrawing too much too soon, the potential problems confronting nonborrowing spouses, and foreclosures for desperate borrowers who could not keep up with their homeowner obligations.

Other matters, however, remain as concerns.

Use Reverse Mortgage Too Quickly for Questionable Expenses

In the past, retirees have opened reverse mortgages to spend the full amount of available credit immediately—perhaps either to overindulge irresponsibly in unnecessary discretionary expenses or to finance shady or even fraudulent investment or insurance products. When considering a reverse mortgage, it is important to be responsible with the strategy and not give in to the temptation to treat the reverse mortgage as a windfall and spend it quickly.

This point cannot be overemphasized, as the natural tendency may be to spend assets as soon as they become liquid. Responsible retirees have little to worry about, but if you lack sufficient self-control, you should handle a reverse mortgage carefully.

Irresponsible borrowers who quickly depleted their assets and suffered later in retirement are part of the reason that reverse mortgages developed their bad reputation. Reverse mortgages were taken out by those who were unable to keep up with their property taxes, homeowner's insurance premiums, and home upkeep. Such defaults triggered foreclosures.

This jeopardized the role of home equity as a reserve asset for the household, and attention has been paid to reducing this risk of misuse.

HUD requires a counseling session and includes a financial assessment to make sure that sufficient resources will be available to meet homeowner obligations related to keeping a reverse mortgage in place. Set-asides can be carved into the credit capacity to ensure payment of future property taxes and other homeowner obligations if other resources are not available.

Furthermore, fixed-rate HECMs, which were more common in the past, required taking the entire borrowing capacity at the start, creating a greater risk that these funds would be spent in irresponsible ways. Today there are limits on how much of the principal limit or borrowing capacity can be accessed in the first year.

The initial disbursement limit during the first year is now the greater of 60 percent of the initial principal limit, or the total of mandatory obligations plus a further 10 percent of the initial principal limit. Mandatory obligations include repayments on any outstanding mortgage balances when the loan is initiated (see Chapter 6 for this strategy), closing costs, initial mortgage insurance premiums, other liens or judgments affecting the home, federal debt, or set-asides for repairs or other homeowner obligations during the first year of the loan. The remainder of the principal limit will become fully available for a variable-rate loan as of the second year of the loan. Fixed rate loans do not have a line of credit.

Since 2015, a financial assessment has also been required to ensure that the borrower has the capacity to make these payments. If other resources are not available, set-asides will be carved out of the line of credit to support these payments. These do not become part of the loan balance until they are spent, but they do otherwise limit the amount that you can borrow from the line of credit. Nonetheless, to the extent that the liquidity from the reverse mortgage leads to a behavioral issue of overspending, this is a concern for potential borrowers with limited self-control.

Family Misunderstandings

The media has reported on adult children who are surprised to find that they will not inherit the house after their parents passed away because their parents used a reverse mortgage. Such media reports are typically based on misunderstandings on the part of angry children. Articles focus on only one aspect of inheritance (the home) and do not consider how to best meet the retirement spending needs of parents. Children can pay the loan balance and keep the home, and I will describe how strategic use of a reverse mortgage to cover a fixed retirement spending need is *more* likely to increase the overall amount of legacy wealth available to children at the end. One must also consider whether the parents' assets were best used to meet their own spending goals or to provide a legacy for their children.

Foreclosure

Foreclosures for the elderly, generated by the inability to meet technical requirements of the loan, generated negative media coverage and a misconstruing of the HECM program. These types of stories can still be found occasionally. New safeguards have been added, but it is important to keep in mind that such retirements were not sustainable in the first place. Reverse mortgages may still have created net-positive impacts for these households, as their living situations could have otherwise worsened much sooner.

For reverse mortgages, monthly repayments are not required, so nonpayment of the loan does not trigger foreclosure. The foreclosure is typically triggered by not paying property taxes or not meeting another homeowner obligation that exists regardless of whether a reverse mortgage is used. Reverse mortgages may have helped delay what was ultimately inevitable, allowing you to maintain a higher quality of life in your own home for longer than otherwise possible before reaching this stage of end-of-life poverty. Media coverage on this point often emphasizes the problems created by foreclosure without considering whether the reverse mortgage provided a positive impact and prolonged the arrival of this inevitability.

Nonborrowing Spouses

In the past, younger spouses were taken off a home's title to allow a reverse mortgage to proceed, only to be surprised when the borrower died and the nonborrowing spouse either had to repay the loan or leave the home. Since 2015, protections are in place for nonborrowing spouses in all states but Texas. Though nonborrowing spouses cannot continue to borrow funds from the line of credit, these spouses who are deemed eligible can remain in the home even after the borrowing spouse has passed away, without worrying about loan repayment, until they also leave the home on their own volition. As of 2021, eligible nonborrowing spouses are also protected if the borrower must leave the home for medical reasons, such as needing long-term care in an institutional setting. Lending limits will be based on the younger eligible spouse's age, to help protect the insurance fund.

Home Title

There is a common misconception that the lender receives the title to the home as part of a reverse mortgage. This enduring myth about the HECM program is simply untrue and was *never* true.

HECM 4 Nevers

In her book, *What's the Deal with Reverse Mortgages?*, Shelley Giordano describes what she calls the "HECM 4 Nevers" to help dispel common misconceptions about the program. She clarifies that homeowners never give up the title to their home; never owe more than the home's value upon leaving the home; never have to leave the home due to spending down their line of credit, as long as taxes, insurance, and home maintenance continue; and never have to make loan repayments in advance of leaving the home, unless they choose to do so.

High Costs

In the past, the initial costs for opening reverse mortgages could be as high as 6 percent of the home value. These upfront costs have been reduced dramatically for competitive lenders. Nonetheless, HECM loans originated today include an unavoidable 2 percent upfront mortgage insurance premium. That adds up to $2,000 per $100,000 of appraised home value. Other closing costs for home appraisal, titling, and other matters cannot be avoided, and there are loan origination fees with maximum thresholds that cannot be exceeded (the next chapter provides more details). Consumers may shop around to see what is offered by different lenders. These costs can create an initial "sticker shock," but the analysis in this book will demonstrate how the benefits can exceed the costs for retirees by improving their overall outcomes in terms of spending and legacy. The initial "sticker price" then becomes a psychological barrier to obtaining a better overall outcome for the retirement.

Taxpayer Risk

Though many reforms have been taken to further protect the government's mortgage insurance fund from claims related to the non-recourse aspects of reverse mortgages, some individuals may still worry about this taxpayer risk. Reduced housing prices in the 2000s created problems that would be addressed with the Reverse Mortgage Stabilization Act of 2013, which helped make sure insurance premiums and lending limits were sufficient to keep the insurance fund self-sustaining. Further action was taken with rules implemented on October 2, 2017, which increase initial mortgage insurance premiums and reduce initial borrowing amounts and growth rates on the line of credit. These actions have further reduced the risks for the mortgage insurance fund.

Stigma About Using Debt

Psychologically, some may be challenged by the idea of using a debt instrument in retirement after having spent their careers working to reduce their debt. This is merely a psychological constraint. If you think about your investment portfolio and home equity as assets, then meeting spending goals requires spending from assets somewhere on the retirement balance sheet. In this regard, spending from home equity does not necessarily need to be framed as accumulating debt any more than does spending from investment assets. A reverse mortgage creates liquidity for an otherwise illiquid asset. Though a reverse mortgage loan balance is a debt, it is different from traditional debt since it does not include an ongoing, fixed repayment obligation. Spending from home equity reduces the subsequent available home equity in the same way that spending from investments reduces the subsequent value of the investment portfolio. Repayment happens at the end and is limited by the value of the home at that time, which is a protection not afforded to an investment portfolio. Nonetheless, we must acknowledge that this psychological constraint will reflect a barrier for HECM use that will be difficult to overcome for some individuals.

A Brief History of Reverse Mortgages in the United States

Reverse mortgages have a relatively short history in the United States. The first was issued by a bank in Maine in 1961. The 1987 Housing and Community Development Act saw the federal government systemize reverse mortgages through the Home Equity Conversion Mortgage (HECM) program, under the auspices of the US Department of Housing and Urban Development (HUD). Since that time, about 1.3 million HECMs have been initiated, and there were about 400,000 active HECMs at the end of October 2022.

I intend to focus on HECM reverse mortgages, which are tightly regulated and represent the bulk of reverse mortgages. I will not be discussing programs such as those offered through local governments to provide liquidity for a more limited purpose, or proprietary reverse mortgages, which may appeal to those with homes worth more than the $1,089,300 FHA lending limit (as of January 1, 2023, and subject to change). A HECM can be obtained on homes worth more than $1,089,300, but the funds available through the reverse mortgage will be based on the lesser of the home's appraised value or $1,089,300.

In recent years, HUD has frequently updated the administration of the HECM program to address various issues and ensure that reverse mortgages are used responsibly. As a result, descriptions of the program can quickly become outdated, even if they are only a couple of years old. While older materials may explain the concepts adequately, they might be missing key changes. As of January 2023, the most recent major program changes went into effect on October 2, 2017. Anything published before that date does not reflect important characteristics of the program for new loan applications.

Lender standards have tightened, and the number of new reverse mortgages issued has declined after peaking at around 110,000 per year in 2008 and 2009. Many borrowers at the peak were financially constrained and unable to keep up with taxes, insurance, and home maintenance. Among those who borrowed, many opted to take out the full available initial credit amount as a lump sum. After spending this down quickly, they were left with no other assets, which led to many foreclosures. On top of that, falling home prices meant that many loan balances exceeded the value of the homes being used as collateral when repayment was due, which put greater pressure on the mortgage insurance fund.

Exhibit 3.1 provides statistics on HECM usage since 2012. The number of new HECMs each year had stabilized at around 50,000 before picking up in 2022 as part of increased interest during the financial market downturn. In the past several years, we can observe a rise in refinancing as growing home prices and declining interest rates created greater borrowing capacity. The

HECM for Purchase program that can be used as part of purchasing a new home continues to have uptake, but it is not a widely used program yet. This exhibit also highlights the reversal from the fixed-rate option (which does not have a line of credit) to the variable- or adjustable-rate option that does have a line of credit. The adjustable-rate option, which is the primary focus here, is the choice for more than 90 percent of new HECM issues.

Exhibit 3.1
Historical Home Equity Conversion Mortgage (HECM) Usage

| | | Loan Type | | | Product Type | |
	Total Endorsement Count	HECM for Purchase	Refinance	Equity Takeout (Traditional)	Fixed Rate	Adjustable Rate
FY 2022	64,440	3.5%	45.0%	51.6%	4.4%	95.6%
FY 2021	49,195	4.5%	42.0%	53.5%	7.2%	92.8%
FY 2020	41,824	5.9%	20.6%	73.5%	1.9%	98.1%
FY 2019	31,272	7.3%	5.4%	87.3%	6.0%	94.0%
FY 2018	48,329	5.4%	12.1%	82.5%	10.1%	89.9%
FY 2017	55,292	4.8%	14.5%	80.7%	10.4%	89.6%
FY 2016	48,865	4.8%	11.0%	84.1%	10.6%	89.4%
FY 2015	57,990	4.2%	9.6%	86.2%	15.7%	84.3%
FY 2014	51,617	3.5%	4.7%	91.8%	25.2%	74.8%
FY 2013	59,917	3.5%	3.1%	93.4%	60.6%	39.4%
FY 2012	54,677	3.0%	2.5%	94.6%	69.5%	30.5%

Source: Various FHA Production Reports
(https://www.hud.gov/program_offices/housing/hsgrroom/fhaprodrpt)
Note: Fiscal year runs from October 1 to September 30.

Many older resources on reverse mortgages describe two versions: the HECM Standard and HECM Saver. The HECM Saver was introduced in October 2010 as a contrast to HECM Standard and in response to increased foreclosures. It provided access to a smaller percentage of the home's value, substantially reducing borrowers' mortgage insurance premiums. It represented a step toward encouraging less upfront use of reverse mortgage credit, but it went largely unused. By September 2013, the Saver and Standard merged back into a single HECM option. The newly merged program provides an initial credit amount that is slightly larger than that of the HECM Saver but substantially less than the HECM Standard. Principal limit factors (more on these in Chapter 4) were recalculated to lower available borrowing amounts.

The government also sought to encourage deliberate, conservative use of home equity by implementing penalties and limits. If more than 60 percent of the initial line of credit was spent during the first year, the borrower was charged a higher upfront mortgage insurance premium on the home's appraised value (2.5 percent instead of 0.5 percent). For a $500,000 home with a $237,500 principal limit, the initial mortgage insurance premium jumped from $2,500 to $12,500 if more than $142,500 was spent from the line of credit in year one—a $10,000 incentive to lower spending. In addition, borrowing more than 60 percent of the principal limit was only allowed for qualified mandatory obligations such as paying down an existing mortgage or using the HECM for Purchase program.

Before September 2013, the HECM Standard mortgage had an initial mortgage insurance premium of 2 percent of the home value, so the upfront costs for opening a reverse mortgage dropped significantly for those who could stay under the 60 percent limit, after HECM Standard and Saver merged. Yet they still paled in comparison to the HECM Saver, as the new 0.5 percent upfront mortgage premium was considerably higher than the previous 0.01 percent value. So, while the new rules were designed to encourage more gradual and deliberate HECM use, the costs for setting up this opportunity increased, relative to the HECM Saver.

Two important additional consumer safeguards came into full effect in 2015. The first relates to new protections for nonborrowing spouses who don't meet the minimum age 62 requirement. In the past, when one spouse was too young, the solution was typically to remove that spouse from the house title. This created a problem when the borrowing spouse died first and the loan balance came due. Without sufficient liquidity or the ability to refinance, the nonborrowing spouse could be forced out of the home.

HUD implemented safeguards for nonborrowing spouses in 2014 and further clarified them the following year. As of spring 2015, eligible nonborrowing spouses now have the right to stay in the home after the borrower dies or leaves, as the loan balance only needs to be paid after the nonborrowing spouse has also left the home. To be eligible, the nonborrowing spouse must have been the spouse when the loan was closed; must be named as a nonborrowing spouse; must continue to occupy the property as a primary residence; and must maintain the usual taxes, insurance, and home upkeep. These protections apply for loans initiated after August 2014.

While nonborrowing spouses may stay in the home, they are not borrowers. Once the borrower has left the home, there is no further ability to spend from the line of credit, and any term or tenure payments stop. However, interest and mortgage insurance premiums continue to accrue on any outstanding loan balance. After 2014, the new rules initially contained an important caveat: the nonborrower was only protected in the event of the borrower's death. This potential risk for the nonborrowing spouse was alleviated with a new protection from HUD issued in 2021: eligible nonborrowing spouses on loans initiated after August 2014 can now remain in the home even if the borrower leaves the home for a long-term stay in a health-care facility.

The principal limit factors (PLFs) published on August 4, 2014, accounted for nonborrowing spouses. PLFs are now provided for ages 18 and older to account for nonborrowing spouses who are significantly younger than the borrower. Before these changes, PLFs were only needed for ages 62 and older. The PLF is based on the younger of the borrower and eligible nonborrowing spouse.

Though nonborrowing spouses cannot spend from the reverse mortgage, they may remain in the home for many more years, so initial HECM proceeds must be lowered to protect against loan balances exceeding the home's value. Aside from the expansion to account for nonborrowing spouses, the post-August 2014 PLFs underwent further downward revisions to limit the initial available credit amount to ensure that mortgage insurance premiums could cover the risk of loan balances exceeding the home's value.

The other new consumer safeguard implemented in 2014 and effective in 2015 is a more detailed financial assessment for potential borrowers to ensure that they have sufficient means to pay property taxes, homeowner's insurance, maintenance and upkeep, and homeowners' association dues. Determination that potential borrowers will struggle to meet these obligations with assets from outside home equity does not disqualify them from receiving a HECM. Life expectancy set-asides (LESAs) can now be carved out of the principal limit to cover these expenses. Interest on these set-asides does not accrue until the money is spent, but the set-asides prevent borrowers from taking too much from the line of credit and becoming unable to meet the terms required to stay in the home.

Concerns should be raised about the viability of an overall retirement income plan when it is necessary to create large set-asides as part of initiating a HECM. In some cases, a reverse mortgage might simply be a source of liquidity to cover homeowner expenses and allow the borrower to stay in the home while using other limited resources to cover living expenses.

On August 29, 2017, HUD announced a series of new changes to the HECM program parameters for new HECM applications made after October 2, 2017. In Chapter 4, I will explain in full detail what these rules and terms mean, but, briefly, the new rules include:

- The initial mortgage insurance premium when opening a reverse mortgage is now 2 percent of the home value, up to the $1,089,300 lending limit.
- The ongoing mortgage insurance premium on the loan balance is now 0.5 percent.
- A new table of principal limit factors was issued; these generally result in a reduced initial borrowing amount with the reverse mortgage, at least when interest rates are low.
- The floor on the expected rate used to calculate initial borrowing amounts on a reverse mortgage was reduced from 5.06 percent to 3 percent.

Another change issued on September 19, 2017, was to begin allowing nonborrowers to remain on the home title. In the past, only borrowers could remain on the home title. Eligible nonborrowing spouses received protections to be able to stay in the home, but they could not remain on the home title. Now they can, as can any other homeowners, such as siblings or children of the borrower. This creates a new category of ineligible nonborrowers that can remain on the home title today. Any homeowners that wish to remain on the home title must also go through the HECM counseling session and sign some loan documents as part of the borrower's application process. Since these ineligible nonborrowers do not have protections to stay in the home, their ages are not relevant for determining the initial principal limit. Only borrowers or eligible nonborrowing spouses matter for this.

Chapter 4: How Reverse Mortgages Work

The next step toward understanding how reverse mortgages fit into retirement income planning is to see how they work. The following discussion is based on the variable-rate (also known as the adjustable-rate) HECM, which is the only option that includes a line of credit. It became popular after 2013. As shown in Exhibit 3.1 from the previous chapter, variable-rate HECMs accounted for 92.8 percent of HECMs issued in 2021 and 95.6 percent of HECMs issued in 2022.

Other reverse mortgage options include fixed-rate HECMs and proprietary reverse mortgages that exist outside of the HECM program. Fixed-rate HECMs could be considered in cases where a large initial lump sum distribution is desired, without a need for an additional line of credit. I will also describe more about the proprietary options in a separate section later in this chapter. Otherwise, this book is about variable-rate HECMs.

A Point of Emphasis on Fixed and Variable-Rate HECMs

Only the variable-rate (a.k.a. adjustable-rate) HECM offers the line of credit. Fixed-rate HECMs are also available, but these loans do not provide access to additional funds after the initial distribution is taken, except possibly if a specific set-aside is created to cover homeowner obligations. There is no line of credit with the fixed-rate option.

Eligibility Requirements for a HECM Borrower

The basic requirements to become a HECM borrower are:

- age (at least 62),
- equity in your home (any existing mortgage can be refinanced with loan proceeds),
- financial resources to cover tax, insurance, and maintenance,
- no other federal debt,
- competency, and
- receipt of a certificate from an FHA-approved counselor for attending a personal counseling session on home-equity options.

HUD provides a list of approved counselors on its website.

For your *property* to be eligible, it must:

- serve as your primary residence,
- meet FHA property standards and flood requirements,
- be an FHA-eligible property type (this includes single-family homes, two-to-four unit homes with one unit occupied by the borrower, HUD-approved condominium projects, and manufactured homes meeting FHA requirements),
- pass an FHA appraisal, and
- be maintained to meet FHA health and safety standards.

If your home does not meet all standards, some home improvements may also be required. The obligations to pay property taxes, homeowner's insurance, and home maintenance should not be viewed as extraordinary, as they are required for any type of mortgage, not just the reverse types. This protects the lender by maintaining the value of the collateral.

The Initial Principal Limit: Measuring Available Credit

Reverse mortgages use their own jargon, and it is important to understand the meaning of three key terms: (1) principal limit factor (PLF), (2) expected rate, and (3) effective rate. The last two terms sound similar but are not.

The *principal limit* represents the credit capacity available with a HECM reverse mortgage. We need to understand how to calculate the initial principal limit when the reverse mortgage is opened, as well as how the principal limit grows over time. The initial principal limit is calculated with the *expected rate,* while principal limit growth is calculated with the *effective rate.*

PLFs are published by HUD; the current PLF table applies for loans with FHA case numbers assigned on or after October 2, 2017. Because HECMs are non-recourse loans, the principal limit that can be borrowed must be less than the home's value to reduce the potential for the loan balance to outgrow it. Factors are updated over time to manage the risk to the insurance fund.

The basic idea behind reverse mortgages is that the value of the home will eventually be used to repay the loan balance. While the loan balance occasionally ends up exceeding the home's value, the program would be unsustainable if this happened frequently. If the loan balance exceeds the home's appraised value when the loan comes due, the insurance fund makes up the difference to protect both the borrower and lender (an important reason that insurance premiums exist).

The principal limit credit amount is determined primarily by:

- the appraised home value,
- the homeowner's age (or, for couples, the age of the younger eligible spouse—and one spouse must be at least 62),
- a lender's margin, and
- the 10-year Treasury rate.

The lender's margin and the Treasury rate sum to the *expected rate*.

Expected Rate = 10-year Treasury rate + lender's margin

The lender's margin rate charged on the loan balance is the primary way that the lender—or any buyer on the secondary market—earns revenue, especially lenders who have forgone the origination and servicing fees.

The PLF determines the borrowing amount as a percentage of the appraised home value, up to the FHA mortgage limit of $1,089,300. The expected rate is meant to estimate a series of shorter-term interest rates compounded over the next ten years, which provides an estimate for the future path of effective rates. The expected rate is used with the age of the younger spouse to determine the PLF, or the percentage of the home's appraisal value that may be borrowed. If the home's appraisal value exceeds the FHA mortgage limit, this serves as a maximum to which the PLF is applied.

It is important to note that the meaning of the term *age* is a bit more complicated than just a homeowner's literal age; it is rounded up if your birthday falls within 6 months of the first day of the month in which the loan is closed. For instance, say that someone is 65 years old when his or her loan closes during April. Six months after April 1 is October 1. If this person turns 66 by the end of September, his or her age is counted as 66 for the purposes of determining the PLF. But if the borrower's next birthday is in October or later, the age used for determining the principal limit is 65. To clarify, this matter applies after reaching age 62. For the purpose of initiating a loan, someone over age 61.5 does not get to round up to 62.

Exhibit 4.1
Principal Limit Factors—Percentage of Home Value Initially Available

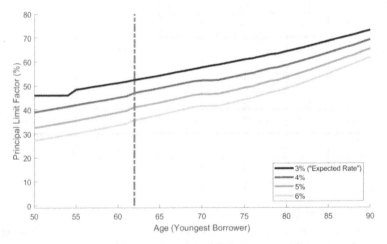

Exhibit 4.1 provides a visual for how these PLFs vary by age and expected rates. Though the range for expected rates is now allowed to vary from 3 percent to 18.875 percent, the exhibit shows only the lower end of the

spectrum, which has been more relevant in recent years. The percentage of home value increases when the age of the youngest borrower or nonborrowing spouse is higher and when the expected rate is lower. The PLF is based on a present-value calculation; more can be provided initially when the time horizon is shorter (i.e., the person is older) and when the interest rate is lower.

A lower interest rate provides an advantage when opening a reverse mortgage, as the PLF is higher. Interest rates are quite important relative to age. For example, with an expected rate of 5 percent, the PLF is 41 percent when the youngest eligible borrower is 62. However, should the rate rise to 6 percent, the youngest borrower would have to be 69 before the PLF again reaches 41 percent. In this case, it takes 7 years for the age impact to offset a one percentage point rise in interest rates.

Because the expected rate is so important for determining initial borrowing amounts, a future increase in interest rates could work to counteract any benefits from an increasing age in determining the PLF for a new reverse mortgage contract. Exhibit 4.2 provides a similar perspective, but with age and expected rates swapped on the horizontal axis. Again, we observe lower principal-limit factors when expected rates are higher. Increasing ages support higher principal-limit factors across the range of expected rates.

Exhibit 4.2
Principal Limit Factors—Percentage of Home Value Initially Available

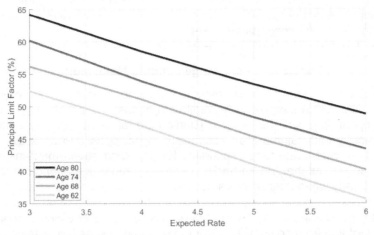

The PLF is the percentage of the home's value initially available. If the principal limit then grows at the expected rate thereafter, it is expected to grow to equal the appreciated home value when the loan comes due (either upon death or leaving the home).

For example, the PLF is 41 percent when the youngest borrower is 62 and the expected rate is 5 percent. The government's specific assumptions are not provided publicly, but if we assume a 2 percent growth rate for home appreciation and a remaining life expectancy of 31 years, to age 93, then we can replicate the actual value for the PLF. A home appreciation rate of 2.57 percent combined with a life expectancy to 100 (38 years) also makes the calculation work for the principal limit to equal the home value at that time.

The government might use a different combination of values for these two variables, but this formula shows the basic idea of how the PLF is calculated:

$$PLF = \left(\frac{1 + \text{home value growth rate}}{1 + \text{expected rate}} \right)^{\text{remaining life expectancy}}$$

Upfront Costs for Opening a Reverse Mortgage

Upfront costs for reverse mortgages come in three categories.

1. *Origination fee.* First, the mortgage lender can charge an origination fee. Under the HECM program, these fees are currently permitted to be up to 2 percent of the value for homes worth $200,000 or less, or $2,500 if this value is greater. For homes worth between $200,000 and $400,000, the maximum allowed origination fee is $4,000 plus 1 percent of the home's value above $200,000. For homes worth more than $400,000, the maximum origination fee is $6,000. These fees are the maximum allowed by the government. Lenders have discretion to reduce or waive these fees, and they may even offer credits for other fees. These lenders may either charge higher lender margins to offset the fee reductions or earn revenue primarily by originating loans to sell on the secondary market.

How Reverse Mortgage Lenders Make Money

Readers may wonder how reverse mortgage lenders make money, especially in cases where they credit upfront costs for initiating a HECM. One option is to sell the loans to Ginnie Mae for more than the value of the money lent. Ginnie Mae securitizes these loans and sells them to investors, who value these securities for providing government-insured, risk-free returns that, unlike traditional forward mortgages, tend not to be repaid early when interest rates decline.

Prior to the October 2017 rules change, I saw cases in which companies offered total upfront costs of $125 for the required counseling session with a $0 origination fee, along with credits to cover the mortgage insurance and other closing costs described in the following paragraphs. With the updated initial mortgage insurance premium rule, it is no longer feasible for lenders to provide credits for the full upfront costs. But shopping around will continue to be important.

2. *Initial mortgage insurance premium.* A second source of upfront costs is the initial mortgage insurance premium paid to the government, which is based on the value of the home. It is 2 percent of the home value up to the $1,089,300 lending limit, or a maximum of $21,786.

The purpose of the mortgage insurance premiums is to cover the guarantees provided by the FHA to the lender and borrower. This protection ensures that the borrower has access to the full principal limit even if the lender experiences financial difficulties. The lender is protected from the non-recourse aspect of the loan. If the loan balance exceeds 95 percent of the appraised value of the home, the insurance fund will make up the difference for the lender. This allows borrowers to receive greater access to funds and a growing line of credit that would not be possible without the government guarantees. The government fund also bears the risk with the tenure- and term-payment options, as distributions are guaranteed to continue when the borrower remains eligible, even if the principal limit has been fully tapped.

A Heads-Up on Upfront Costs

When I mention upfront costs, I refer to the full initial costs paid by the borrower at any point. As I noted, the borrower may pay them with other resources or finance them as part of the initial HECM loan balance. Upfront costs can be less than their full retail value, as lenders do not have to charge the origination fee, and they may provide credits for insurance and other closing costs.

Some lenders use a different way to explain initial costs. They will say that there are no "out of pocket" costs with a reverse mortgage. What they mean is just that the borrower can finance the upfront costs as part of the initial HECM loan balance. Upfront costs can still be high; they are just not paid at the beginning.

Upfront costs and out-of-pocket costs can be misinterpreted as meaning the same thing. When I speak of low upfront costs, I mean that credits have been applied to reduce them, not that they are simply financed within the loan to keep out-of-pocket costs low. When speaking with a lender, it is important to understand this distinction. In my case studies for later chapters, I do assume that the upfront costs are financed within the loan so that there are limited out-of-pocket costs.

---

3. *Closing costs.* Finally, there are closing costs common for any type of mortgage. These include the costs of the FHA-mandated counseling session, a home appraisal, credit checks, and any costs related to titling. If the appraisal shows shortcomings of the home that could impact health or safety, then additional home repairs may be required as part of setting up the reverse mortgage. Typical closing costs range from $3,000 to $4,000, though they could vary and be higher in some circumstances. Some lenders

may also provide credits to cover some of these costs. The only exception is that lenders are not allowed to pay for the counseling session.

These upfront costs could be paid from other resources or financed from the proceeds of the reverse mortgage loan and repaid later with interest. If upfront costs are financed, the net PLF is what remains after subtracting these costs. You should plan to stay in your home long enough to justify payment of any upfront costs.

Ongoing Credit and Costs

The ongoing costs for a reverse mortgage relate to the interest accruing on any outstanding loan balance and any servicing fees. Servicing fees can be up to $35 per month, though they are generally now incorporated into a higher lender's margin rate rather than being charged directly to the borrower. Once determined through the PLF, the initial line of credit grows automatically at the effective rate, which is a variable rate updated monthly, equal to the lender's margin, a 0.5 percent mortgage insurance premium (MIP), and subsequent values of 1-month or 1-year Treasury rates, as chosen by the borrower. I will assume a 1-year rate is used.

Effective Rate = 1-year Treasury rate + lender's margin + annual mortgage insurance premium (0.5 percent)

The short-term rates are the only variable part of future growth, as the lender's margin and MIP are set contractually at the onset of the loan.

In January 2023, the 1-year Constant Maturity Treasury Rate was about 4.7 percent, and the 10-year Constant Maturity Treasury Rate was about 3.9 percent. If we assume a 2.5 percent lender's margin, which is presently a reasonable estimate, that gives us an expected rate of 6.4 percent and an effective rate of 7.7 percent.

Expected Rate = 3.9% + 2.5% = 6.4% (for initial principal limit)

Effective Rate: = 4.7% + 2.5% + 0.5% = 7.7% (for principal-limit growth)

To summarize, the expected rate is used to determine the initial principal limit factor, and the effective rate is used determine the ongoing principal limit growth rate, which impacts both loan balance and line-of-credit growth. Costs determined by the lender include origination fees, other closing costs, servicing fees, and the margin rate.

These four ingredients can be combined into different packages by the lender. The best choice depends on how the reverse mortgage is used. When funds will be extracted earlier, it may be worthwhile to pay higher upfront fees coupled with a lower margin rate in order to slow growth of the loan balance. For a standby line of credit that may go untapped, it could be beneficial to lean toward a higher margin rate combined with a package for reduced origination and servicing fees to achieve faster credit growth and lower costs.

There is a catch for those seeking to grow the line of credit. The choice of lender's margin is important because it affects both the initial PLF and the subsequent growth rate of the principal limit. A higher lender's margin reduces the initial principal limit as part of the expected rate, but this principal limit subsequently grows faster, as the margin is also part of the effective rate that determines principal limit growth.

There will be a crossover point when the faster principal limit growth overcomes the lower initial principal limit to provide greater overall borrowing capacity. But this can be difficult to calculate as it depends on current interest rates and how they change, as well as on how the upfront costs can be adjusted in response to accepting different lender's margins. Most reverse mortgage lenders should have software available to help model these different possibilities and to provide a sense of what could happen under different scenarios. Potential borrowers may ask lenders to provide a range of options with different variations for upfront costs and lender's margins.

Spending Options for a Variable-Rate HECM

A reverse mortgage can fit into a retirement income plan in several ways, but it is important to first understand your options for taking distributions from a HECM. Most current HECM reverse mortgages use a variable interest rate, which allows the proceeds from the reverse mortgage to be taken out in any of four ways. As noted, the substantially less popular fixed-rate HECM only allows only for a one-time, upfront, lump-sum distribution option.

The spending options for a variable-rate HECM include:

1. *Lump-sum payment.* One takes out a large amount initially, though not necessarily the full amount available.

2. *Tenure payment.* These work similarly to an income annuity, with a guaranteed fixed monthly payment while the borrower remains in the home (which, to be clear, is not the same as dying, as the borrower may leave the home while still alive or otherwise fail to meet homeowner obligations). Tenure payments allow for additional spending from the HECM even when the line of credit has been fully used. The mortgage insurance fund bears the risk that payouts and loan growth from the tenure-payment option could exceed the subsequent value of the home when the loan is repaid.

For those interested in the mechanics, the available monthly tenure payment can be calculated using the PMT formula in Excel:

=PMT (rate, nper, pv, *0, 1)*

in which:

- *rate* is the expected rate plus the 0.5 percent mortgage insurance premium, all divided by 12 to convert into a monthly amount. This gives us the rate at which the loan balance is expected to grow. For example, a 5 percent expected rate makes this number 5.5 percent/12 = 0.458 percent;
- *nper* is the number of months between the age of the youngest borrower (or eligible nonborrowing spouse) and age 100. For example, a new 62-year-old has 456 months (38 years) until he or she turns 100; and
- *pv* is the net principal limit from the reverse mortgage. It is found by multiplying the principal limit factor by the appraised value of the home (up to $1,089,300), less any mandatory obligations, set-asides, and upfront costs financed with the loan. For instance, a 62-year-old with a $500,000 home and a 41 percent PLF who pays upfront costs from other resources will have a $205,000 net principal limit.

And so, PMT (0.458, 456, 205000, 0, 1) = $1,068 for a monthly tenure payment. This sums to $12,816 per year from the HECM.

3. *Term payment*. This is a fixed monthly payment received for a fixed amount of time. Calculating a term payment is similar to calculating a tenure payment. The only difference is that *nper* is smaller, as it is the desired number of months that the term payment should last. If the number of months pushes the term past age 100, a tenure payment would be used instead. As with a tenure payment, the full amount of term payments will be paid even if rising rates cause the loan balance plus new payments to exceed the principal limit. As an example, consider an 8-year term payment, which could be used as part of a strategy to delay Social Security (see Chapter 7). The monthly term payment would be PMT (0.458, 8*12, 205000, 0, 1) = $2,632, or $31,588 annually. My reverse mortgage calculator, which is described later in this chapter, also provides these calculations for tenure and term payments.

4. *Line of credit*. Home equity does not need to be spent initially—or ever. A reasonable strategy involves opening a line of credit and then leaving it to grow at a variable interest rate as an available resource to cover a variety of contingencies later in retirement. Ad hoc distributions can be taken from the remaining line of credit when desired.

These spending options can be combined. Using a portion of the line of credit to create tenure (or term) payments and leaving the remainder to grow is called "modified tenure" (or "modified term"). You can also change spending options over time, in which case updated term or tenure payments would be based on the available line of credit. Should tenure or term payments begin at a later date, the expected rate used to calculate the initial principal limit would remain the same throughout the term of the loan.

Understanding HECM Line of Credit Growth

A HECM's effective rate is applied not just to the loan balance but also to the overall principal limit, which grows throughout the duration of the loan. How the effective rate is applied may sound technical, but it is an overwhelmingly important point to grasp the concept of credit line growth.

Typically speaking, the principal limit, loan balance, any set-asides, and the remaining line of credit all grow at the same effective rate. The sum of the loan balance, line of credit, and any set-asides is the principal limit. Interest and insurance premiums are charged on the loan balance, not on set-asides or the line of credit. Set-asides are not part of the loan balance until they are actually used, but they limit access to the line of credit. Though interest and insurance premiums are not levied on set-asides or the line of credit, both components grow *as if* interest and premiums were charged.

When funds are borrowed, the line of credit decreases and the loan balance increases. Conversely, voluntary repayments increase the amount of the line of credit as the loan balance decreases. These components will then continue to grow at the effective rate, allowing for access to more credit later.

The following equation shows this relationship, which continues to hold throughout the life of the loan:

Principal Limit = loan balance + available line of credit + set-asides

Exhibit 4.3 expresses the same concept. The overall principal limit consists of the loan balance, remaining line of credit, and any set-asides. Again, all these factors grow at the same effective rate, which increases the size of the overall pie over time. If no further spending or repayment happens over time, the proportions of each of these components of the principal limit remain the same since they all grow at the same rate.

Exhibit 4.3: Components of the Principal Limit

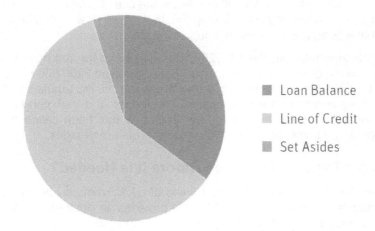

■ Loan Balance

▨ Line of Credit

▩ Set Asides

Having a growing line of credit is a valuable consideration for opening a reverse mortgage sooner than it is needed. It is also a detail that creates a great deal of confusion for those first learning about reverse mortgages, perhaps because it seems that this feature is almost too good to be true.

I believe that the motivation for the government's design of the HECM program is based on an underlying assumption that borrowers will spend from their HECM sooner rather than later. Implicitly, the growth in the principal limit would then reflect growth of the loan balance more than the growth of the line of credit.

The line of credit happens to grow at the same rate as the loan balance. If left unused, it can grow quite large. There was probably never an expectation that such open lines of credit would just be left alone for decades. However, as I will discuss, the bulk of the research on this matter since 2012 suggests that this sort of delayed gradual use of the line of credit can be extremely helpful in sustaining an investment portfolio.

A simple example may help illuminate the concept further. Consider two individuals. Each opens a variable-rate HECM with a principal limit of $100,000. For simplicity's sake, we'll assume that initial disbursement limits do not apply and that the principal limit for both borrowers has grown to $200,000 after 10 years.

Person A takes out the entire $100,000 initially from the reverse mortgage (100 percent of the principal limit is the loan balance). For this person, the $200,000 principal limit after ten years reflects a $200,000 loan balance (the loan balance is still 100 percent of the principal limit), which consists of the initial $100,000 received plus another $100,000 divided between accumulated interest and insurance premiums.

Person B takes a different route and opens the HECM but does not use any of the credit (in practice, a *de minimis* balance is needed to keep the line open), so the $200,000 principal limit at the end of 10 years reflects the line of credit. The principal limit is still 100 percent in the line of credit. This value was calculated with an implicit assumption that interest and insurance payments have been accruing, even though they haven't.

Person B can then take out the full $200,000 after 10 years and have the same loan balance as Person A, but Person B has received $200,000 rather than $100,000. At this point, Person B has bypassed the accumulation of interest and insurance to the detriment of the lender and the mortgage insurance fund. This creative strategy for Person B has been called the "ruthless option" by some academics who study reverse mortgages.

Why Open a Reverse Mortgage Before It Is Needed?

Another question that will arise: Would the line of credit ultimately be larger if opened later rather than earlier? Exhibit 4.4 provides an illustration of the impact of opening a HECM using historical data and a few basic assumptions. This historical data will be described further when the case studies are presented in the next chapter. For now, we can get a sense about the dynamics that lead to the largest borrowing capacity: open the line of credit on a HECM sooner and let it grow, or wait to open to benefit from higher PLF percentages at more advanced ages as well as a hoped-for home appreciation will lead to a larger overall principal limit.

We consider a case study for a couple who recently retired after both celebrated their 62nd birthdays. They own a home appraised at $450,000 with no outstanding mortgage debt. For the HECM, I assume that they pay full upfront costs without any lender credits, to avoid providing any advantage to HECM strategies. At age 62, this includes an origination fee of $6,000, a 2 percent initial mortgage insurance premium of $9,000, and other closing costs of $4,000. This is a combined total cost of $19,000 when the loan is initiated. These costs are financed in the loan balance. I also assume a lender's margin of 2.5 percent for the HECM.

If they wait until later to open a HECM, I assume the other closing costs grow with the consumer price index, and the mortgage insurance premium is 2 percent of the subsequent home value (or the maximum lending limit, which I also assume grows with inflation). I keep the origination fees fixed under the current schedule as they do not automatically adjust.

The initial principal limit will vary over time in the historical data, as the expected rate to determine this value includes the 10-year Treasury rate at the start of that retirement simulation. The subsequent principal limit growth also varies, since it is determined by the sum of the 2.5 percent lender's margin, the ongoing 0.5 percent mortgage insurance, and the variable 1-year Treasury rate.

To analyze these retirement strategies, I use financial market and housing data since 1890 (see the next chapter for more detail). Three variables are relevant to understand about the relationship between the principal limits at various starting ages: the value of the 10-year Treasury rate used to calculate the expected rate when the HECM is opened, the value of 1-year Treasury rates that will guide the subsequent growth of the principal limit and line of credit when opened at 62, and the evolution of the home price if the loan is opened after age 62. With the 1-year variable rate HECM, the effective rate cannot change by more than 5 percentage points from its initial level at the time the loan is initiated. As an example, if the 1-year Treasury is 3 percent on initiation and later rises to 11 percent, the effective rate is calculated using a Treasury rate cap of 8 percent.

Exhibit 4.4 provides the results of this analysis across 100 rolling historical periods in which the individual can be tracked from age 62 to 95. This exhibit shows that, in more than 60 percent of cases, the line of credit on the HECM will be larger when opened at 62 than at a later age. For instance, in 76 percent of the cases, the retiree could have access to a larger line by opening at 62 than by waiting until age 75. The growth of the line of credit as determined through its evolving effective rate in the historical data more than compensated any benefit that could have been derived from waiting for a higher PLF with age, hoping for a lower 10-year Treasury rate to boost the PLF, and hoping to get further benefit through home price appreciation.

Exhibit 4.4
Probability that the Net Principal Limit is Larger at a Subsequent Age When Opened at Age 62 as Compared to Opening at a Later Age

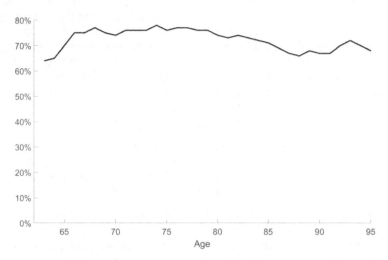

Though not a certainty, Exhibit 4.4 shows that the odds are in favor of having greater borrowing capacity from the HECM by opening it at age 62 as compared to waiting. Two other comments about this may be relevant. First, this analysis assumes that the same rules for the HECM will apply for up to 33 years when the individual waits past age 62. HECM rules do get revised over time, and it is possible that the initial borrowing capacity could be adversely impacted in the future. This would speak to the value of opening the HECM sooner and being locked into the current rules. At the same time, rules could be revised to expand borrowing capacity in the future. In these situations, it is possible to refinance the HECM to further expand your credit.

The other comment relates to protecting the value of the home. In scenarios where the home value stagnates or even declines, opening the HECM sooner will certainly allow for a larger subsequent principal limit. In cases where the home appreciates rapidly, this can contribute to scenarios where the line of credit is larger by waiting to open. Again, those who opened sooner do have the option to refinance their HECM to obtain the higher borrowing capacity that became possible either through declining interest rates or more rapid home appreciation. This is precisely what happened in 2021, as Exhibit 3.1 shows: 43.1 percent of HECM issues that year reflected a refinancing of an existing HECM as housing prices soared and interest rates achieved new lows. The high probabilities shown in Exhibit 4.4 for larger borrowing capacity when opening the HECM sooner, combined with the option to refinance the HECM in other cases, create a compelling argument that those who may wish to use a HECM as part of their retirement strategy may seek to initiate the loan sooner to allow for credit line growth.

A historical scenario we will refer to in detail in the next chapter uses market data from 1962 to 1995. Relevant information for this scenario is provided in Exhibit 4.5. With the historical data, the interpretation is not that the HECM was truly initiated in 1962, as the HECM program did not yet exist. Rather, today's rules for the HECM program are applied to the market data (10-year Treasuries, 1-year Treasuries, and home prices) from 1962 to 1995. In this case, the home appreciates from $450,000 in 1962 to $2.34 million at the end of 1995. A HECM opened at the start of 1995 would result in a net principal limit of $1.27 million as the current lending limit grew with inflation for 33 years. However, had the HECM been initiated at age 62, its net principal limit would have grown to $2.75 million in 1995, which is larger than the home's value at that point. The borrowing capacity would have been larger throughout the life of the loan if the HECM had been initiated at age 62 rather than at a later age.

Exhibit 4.5
Comparing Principal Limits Based on When the Reverse Mortgage Opens
For a 62-Year-Old, Market Data for 1962-1995

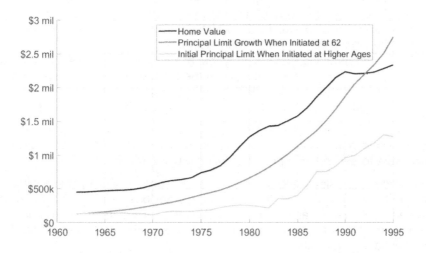

This growing line of credit may sound too good to be true—and it probably is, to some extent. Perhaps this is why it is difficult to grasp the concept of line-of-credit growth throughout retirement. I've already noted that unused lines of credit help borrowers to the detriment of lenders and the government's insurance fund. Such use of a reverse mortgage still exists today and would be contractually protected for those who initiate reverse mortgages under the current rules. I wrote in the first edition that at some point in the future, I expect to see new limitations on line-of-credit growth, especially as more people start to follow the findings of recent research on this matter. A round of such limitations came into effect in October 2017. You should have seen what these exhibits looked like before that rule change! Nevertheless, line of credit growth remains a valuable consideration.

HECM credit growth may be viewed a bit like an unintended loophole. Further limitations on credit growth could potentially be created someday for newly issued loans. Until then, research points to this growth as a valuable way that HECMs can contribute to retirement planning, as I describe in later chapters.

Refinancing a Reverse Mortgage for Better Terms

The rise in popularity of HECM refinancing since 2020 has prompted me to include a new section on this topic. A HECM-to-HECM refinance is possible, with the borrower obtaining a new HECM with the loan balance transferred over from an existing HECM. Several reasons exist for why someone may wish to refinance:

- Rapid home-price appreciation can allow for a larger principal limit and greater borrowing capacity after refinancing. As a related point, the FHA mortgage limit now stands at $1,089,300, and it was $679,650 as recently as 2018. Some more highly valued homes may benefit from refinancing with the larger limit now in place.
- Declining interest rates coupled with advancing age can support a larger principal limit factor, which in turn can help to support greater borrowing capacity after refinancing.
- Other practical factors may be at work, such as the borrower's wishing to include a spouse on the loan, wishing to change from a fixed-rate to variable-rate loan, or wishing to benefit from some other change in HECM program rules that support better borrowing terms.

The first two factors have driven the popularity of refinancing in 2020 and 2021. Rapid home appreciation and declining interest rates allowed past borrowers to expand their principal limit through a refinance.

Refinancing decisions should not be taken lightly because there will be additional upfront costs for the refinance. Additional benefits will need to exceed the costs to make the transaction worthwhile. If the remaining line of credit is already sufficiently large, it may not be worthwhile to refinance for an even larger credit line.

The refinance costs can include an origination fee, traditional closing costs, and a mortgage insurance premium. Borrowers can obtain a break on the mortgage insurance premium, though, with credit provided for the amount paid on the previous HECM. The refinance initial insurance premium is 3 percent of the increase in the initial principal limit obtained with the refinance, less the insurance premium paid on the previous HECM.

Some individuals are now even doing a second refinance, which can create problems for this insurance premium, as the first refinance might have had a small premium, leaving little to be credited on the second refinance. At some point, HUD might adjust this rule to provide the credit for cumulative premiums paid.

HECM Calculator

At **https://www.retirementresearcher.com/reverse-mortgage-calculator**, I have created a calculator that allows users to get a sense of the principal limit available with a variable-rate HECM. The net principal limit is calculated on seven inputs; the amount of cash flow that could be received as a tenure payment for those seeking this option is also provided. An optional eighth input also allows a term-payment amount to be calculated.

The first input is the *Home's Appraised Value.* This value is then compared with the $1,089,300 FHA lending limit to determine the *HECM eligible amount* (the eligible amount is the lesser of the two).

The next two inputs are the current *10-year Treasury Rate* and the *Lender's Margin,* which together comprise the expected rate. The 10-year Treasury rate is automatically updated, so it is not necessary for users to change this value—but the calculator provides flexibility to adjust it if desired.

The next input is the *Age of Youngest Eligible Borrowing or Nonborrowing Spouse.* Remember that those who are within 6 months of their next birthday should use that higher age when determining this input. These four inputs are used to calculate the *Principal Limit Factor.*

Next, inputs for *Loan Origination Fee* and *Other Closing Costs* are combined with the predetermined cost for the *Initial Mortgage Insurance* premium to determine the total upfront loan cost.

The next input asks for the *Percentage of Upfront Costs to be Financed* by the loan. This would be 0 percent if costs are financed from other resources, 100 percent if fully financed by the loan, or any number in between.

The final input is the amount of *Debt Repayment, Repairs, or Other Life-Expectancy Set-Aside Requirements (LESA)* that have been determined as part of the borrower's financial assessments. This information about costs and set-asides is then applied to the eligible home value and the PLF to calculate the net available HECM credit with the loan.

Finally, the calculator provides the net amounts available as either tenure or term payments. The tenure payment is calculated assuming a planning age of 100 and the expected rate plus the ongoing mortgage insurance premium (0.5 percent). The term payment is calculated for a fixed term, though if the desired number of years for the term payment should extend beyond age 100, the term payment is automatically adjusted to be the higher value of the tenure payment. Tenure and term payments are both provided as monthly and annual values, and the tenure payment is also represented as a payout rate based on a percentage of the net principal limit plus the financed upfront costs, for those wishing to think in terms of payout rates on income annuities.

Repayment of the HECM Loan Balance

Repayment of a HECM loan balance may be deferred until the last borrower or eligible nonborrowing spouse no longer meets the terms for maintaining the loan, either through death, moving or selling the home, or failing to maintain the homeowner's obligations such as paying property taxes. Prior to that time, repayments can be made voluntarily at any point, with no penalty for early repayment, to help reduce future interest due and allow for a larger line of credit to grow for subsequent use.

Again, the HECM is a non-recourse loan. The borrower (or borrower's estate) is not obligated to pay the lender more than the smaller of the loan balance or 95 percent of the home's appraised value at that time. When the final repayment is due, the title for the home remains with the borrower or estate. Should beneficiaries wish to keep the home, the smaller of the loan balance or 95 percent of the appraised home value can be repaid with other funds. Heirs can also refinance the home with a traditional mortgage, should they wish to keep it. If they qualify, heirs might also consider a new HECM to cover the existing loan balance. If they decide to sell the home, they keep anything beyond the outstanding loan balance. Should the loan balance exceed what the home can reasonably be sold for, heirs can simply give the home to the lender through a deed in lieu of foreclosure, without worrying about selling it themselves. However, they may be sacrificing a large interest deduction on their taxes if they do this and the HECM was used for acquisition debt; they should consult a tax professional first.

A deed in lieu of foreclosure is sufficient to extinguish the debt on the reverse mortgage; mortgage insurance from the government will compensate the lender for the difference. Generally, the borrower or heirs have up to 360 days to sell the home or refinance after the loan comes due, but this requires a few extensions from the lender. If you intend to use the full 360 days, it is essential that you maintain regular contact and provide updates to the lender.

Tax Issues

There are several different tax issues to consider with HECMs. Some of them are quite complex, and it is important to consult with a tax professional with reverse mortgage experience to get the best advice about your personal situation. I am only describing some basic principles to keep in mind.

The first issue is easy. Distributions from reverse mortgages are treated as loan advances and are not taxable income. Just like Roth IRA distributions, HECM proceeds are not included in adjusted gross income and do not impact Medicare premiums or Social Security benefits taxation. HECMs increase spending power without creating more taxable income.

HECM distributions may impact eligibility for means-tested government welfare programs such as Medicaid or Supplemental Security Income. HECMs may reduce benefit eligibility by creating more countable assets as funds are shifted from home equity to a bank account. This is a relevant consideration for those in a "last resort" scenario with limited other assets.

A more complex area relates to tax deductions for reverse mortgages. These taxation issues for reverse mortgages are still relatively untested and not fully addressed in the tax code. Researchers Barry Sacks and Tom Davison have been exploring deeper into the tax code to better understand these aspects. Individual cases vary, so always consult with a professional.

Interest charges and real-estate taxes paid through a set-aside may be accumulated as part of the loan balance and may be left un-repaid until many years later. These are all potentially deductible at different points in time, either as they are incurred or when repaid.

Davison has spent a good deal of time exploring IRS publications about these issues, which he has written up at his *Tools for Retirement Planning* blog. He notes that interest cannot generally be deducted until it is actually repaid. Interest payments include interest charged on the borrowed amount and interest compounded on past interest charged. These two aspects of interest may be treated differently for taxes, as interest on interest is not addressed in tax rules. Barry Sacks and his co-authors take the position in their 2016 article (see further reading) that only the simple interest on the debt can be deductible, and that interest on interest is not deductible. There are also limits on how much interest can be treated as deductible.

Mortgage interest is only tax deductible if the borrowing reflects acquisition debt. This is a reverse mortgage use for buying, building, or substantially improving a home. The HECM for Purchase program, as well as major home-improvement projects, should qualify under this criterion. Refinancing acquisition debt with a reverse mortgage also counts for this purpose, such as when a reverse mortgage is used to refinance a traditional mortgage that was used to purchase the home. Since 2018, interest deductions are no longer allowed for home equity loan debt taken for other purposes.

Repayments on the loan balance are first applied to mortgage insurance premiums, then servicing fees (if any), then interest, then principal amounts borrowed. So repayment cannot lead to interest deductions until the MIP and servicing-fee components have been fully repaid. For voluntary repayments during the life of the loan, one may strategize around bunching repayments that cover interest. This is relevant if it is for acquisition debt, in particular years, to have a portion exceed the standard deduction, so that a true tax deduction benefit can be applied.

Interest due on the loan balance can be large, so this is an important aspect of tax planning; make sure that repayment timing allows for the best use of this deduction when that interest reflects acquisition debt. It is possible that interest repayment could be coupled with an IRA distribution or Roth conversion to generate enough taxable income to avoid losing a portion of a potentially large tax deduction that otherwise exceeds income.

In cases when real-estate taxes are paid from the line of credit, perhaps with a life-expectancy set-aside requirement, any deduction for these taxes should happen as they are incurred rather than when repaid.

A final tax matter relates to the non-recourse aspects of the loan. When the HECM loan balance exceeds 95 percent of the appraised home value, the borrower is not responsible for paying the difference. However, it is possible that this debt forgiveness could be treated as a taxable event. Individuals should consult with a qualified tax professional to understand if there are any potential tax implications when benefiting from the non-recourse aspects of an underwater loan.

Traditional Home Equity Line of Credit vs. HECM

Either a traditional home-equity line of credit (HELOC—pronounced "he-lock") or a HECM can serve as a source for contingency funds in retirement, but they cannot be combined on a given home. People often think that they should just use a HELOC and not bother with a HECM, but there are important differences between the two options. These must be considered before you take either.

With a HELOC, repayments are required sooner. Users of a HECM can voluntarily repay sooner but are under no obligation to make any repayment while maintaining loan eligibility.

In addition, retirees may not qualify for a HELOC if they do not have regular income. Though HECMs added new safeguards in 2015 to make sure that they are not used solely as a last resort by those who have otherwise depleted their resources, the qualification requirements are less stringent than for a HELOC. A HECM may still be available with set-asides included to cover tax, insurance, and maintenance obligations. In addition, initial start-up costs may differ for the two options.

A HECM also differs from a HELOC in that its line of credit cannot be canceled, frozen, or reduced. This was a large problem with HELOCs during the 2008 financial crisis, and the issue arose again during the market panic that accompanied the global pandemic in spring 2020. With a HECM, borrowers are protected from lenders' modifying their obligations to lend remaining funds in the line of credit. HECM funds have to be wired to the individual within 5 business days. No such protections are available with HELOCs. And the principal limit for a HECM will grow throughout retirement, unlike the fixed amount available with a HELOC.

In contrast to a HELOC, the HECM is noncancelable; the borrower controls when it is used; it has flexible payback control; and the line of credit grows over time independent of home value. If your goal is to set up a liquid contingency fund, make sure that you examine the number of important differences between HECMs and HELOCs.

Proprietary Reverse Mortgages

We conclude this chapter with a brief look at proprietary options existing outside of the HECM program. These have been around for years, but recent new product developments may increase their popularity at the present.

The non-recourse aspect of the HECM program, backed by the federal government's mortgage insurance fund, provides valuable insurance for both borrowers and lenders. From the lender's perspective, less risk is taken with issuing a HECM because the lender can expect to be made whole by the insurance fund if the loan balance exceeds the home value.

Without this protection, lenders are less willing to make non-recourse loans. Such loans might have lower borrowing capacities or use higher interest rates to reflect risks to the lender for experiencing a loss when the non-recourse aspect applies.

Nonetheless, another recent trend in the reverse mortgage world is that different proprietary reverse mortgage options are gaining traction and may provide a valuable alternative for more individuals.

These proprietary options are generally offered by the same lenders who offer HECMs. We will consider a few key advantages and disadvantages of these proprietary options. Advantages include:

- Loan capacity may be higher, which may allow for more support for homes valued above the FHA limits. With some options, principal limits can be as high as $4 million on homes valued at $10 million.
- Options exist for borrowers younger than 62. This matter varies on a state-by-state basis, but some states allow for borrowers as young as 55 or 60 for these proprietary options.
- Proprietary options may be available on primary residences that are not otherwise eligible for a HECM.
- Some proprietary options may not require all existing liens to be paid off at closing, such that it may be possible to maintain a traditional mortgage but to use the reverse mortgage to cover those mortgage payments to free up other available cash.
- Any reverse mortgage in the United States must be non-recourse. Major proprietary options also offer many of the same protections to the borrower as the HECM, such as the ability to make voluntary payments, or to not be required to repay the loan until leaving the home or failing to maintain basic homeowner obligations.
- As proprietary loans, these reverse mortgages exist outside of mortgage insurance, and the lack of mortgage insurance premiums can help to reduce upfront costs.

Disadvantages for proprietary options relative to the HECM program include:

- Though the lack of mortgage insurance premiums helps to lower costs, overall costs may still be higher because of larger origination fees and higher lender margins.
- Though borrowing capacity may be higher for highly valued homes, the principal limit percentage of a home value will generally be less than with a comparable HECM for a home under the FHA limit.
- Proprietary options generally do not offer a line of credit, though this is changing. One prominent option now includes a reusable line of credit of up to 75 percent of the loan's principal limit, growing at a 1.5 percent rate for 7 years and available for the first 10 years of the loan. This is clearly less generous than the HECM line of credit, but it is a step in the direction of offering greater flexibility, which is more difficult for the lender without the mortgage insurance to cover any difference when the loan balance exceeds the home value. Lenders take that risk with proprietary options.
- Proprietary options must be approved on a state-by-state basis, so not all options are available in every state.

Especially for those who do not qualify for the HECM program, either because of age or the type of home owned, or who own homes worth significantly more than the FHA limit ($1,089,300), a proprietary reverse mortgage may be an option worth exploring. But it is important to fully understand the terms, costs, and limitations of the loan relative to the HECM program. This section has only provided a brief introduction.

Chapter 5: Portfolio Coordination Strategies

We are now ready to explore the use of HECMs within a retirement plan. Maintaining higher fixed expenses in retirement increases exposure to sequence-of-return risk by requiring a higher withdrawal rate from assets. Drawing from a reverse mortgage has the potential to mitigate this aspect of sequence risk by reducing the need for portfolio withdrawals, either generally (with a tenure payment) or specifically at inopportune times (with a portfolio coordination strategy). Since 2012, numerous research articles have highlighted how the strategic use of a reverse mortgage can either preserve greater overall legacy wealth for a given spending goal or sustain a higher spending amount for longer in retirement. Coordinating distributions from a HECM line of credit with distributions from an investment portfolio can be an effective way to help manage the sequence risk in retirement.

The conventional wisdom on how to treat housing wealth in retirement was to preserve it as a last-resort asset for when all else has failed. But various explorations have shown that the failure to coordinate home equity with the investment portfolio or to attach a growing line of credit to home equity leads to less efficient retirement outcomes. A HECM line of credit provides a tool for mitigating the impacts of sequence-of-return risk. This chapter explores this conclusion in greater depth, to provide more insight about coordinating home equity in a retirement income plan.

Foundational Research on Coordinated Spending

Starting in 2012, a series of articles published in the *Journal of Financial Planning* investigated how obtaining a HECM reverse mortgage early in retirement and then strategically spending from the available credit can help improve the sustainability of retirement income strategies.

We can think of legacy wealth at death as the combined value of any remaining financial assets plus the remaining home equity once the reverse mortgage loan balance has been repaid.

If we do not worry about the percentage breakdown between the investment balance and home equity, research reveals the possibility of sustaining a spending goal while also leaving a larger legacy at death. The investment balance increases by more than the home equity decreases. Strategically using home equity can lead to a more efficient strategy than the less flexible option of viewing the home as the legacy asset that must not be touched until no other options remain for supporting retirement spending.

This analysis provides a way to test whether the costs of the reverse mortgage—in terms of the upfront costs and compounding growth of the loan balance—are outweighed by the benefits of mitigating sequence risk. Strategic use of a HECM line of credit is shown to improve retirement sustainability, without adversely impacting legacy wealth, because the gains from reducing spending pressure on the investment portfolio exceed the costs of the reverse mortgage.

Based on his personal research going as far back as 2004, Barry Sacks got the ball rolling and received widespread recognition for ideas presented in a research article he published with his brother Stephen in the February 2012 issue of the *Journal of Financial Planning*. He had been thinking for a decade about how people could use housing wealth as a type of volatility buffer to help mitigate sequence-of-return risk. The aptly named article these brothers wrote—"Reversing the Conventional Wisdom: Using Home Equity to Supplement Retirement Income"—set out to present the reverse mortgage option as something more than a last resort.

The title states their objective clearly. They investigated sustainable withdrawal rates from an investment portfolio coupled with home equity to determine whether asset depletion takes place in any of three different strategies for incorporating home equity into the retirement income plan:

1. Use a reverse mortgage as a last resort, after the investment portfolio is depleted (i.e., the conventional wisdom).

2. Open a reverse mortgage line of credit at the start of retirement and spend it down first, then transition to using portfolio withdrawals for the remainder of retirement.

3. Open a reverse mortgage line of credit at the start of retirement and draw from it in years following a year with a negative return for the investment portfolio. This is their "coordinated strategy."

They reversed the conventional wisdom by using randomized market returns through Monte Carlo simulations to quantify how spending strategies (2) and (3) enjoyed a higher probability for success and could sustain assets longer.

They also found that the remaining net worth of the household (the value of the remaining financial portfolio plus any remaining home equity) after thirty years of retirement is larger in 67 percent to 75 percent of cases with the coordinated strategy as opposed to the conventional wisdom of saving home equity to be used as a last resort for withdrawal-rate goals between 4.5 percent and 7 percent of the initial retirement portfolio balance. In other words, spending home equity did not ruin the possibility for leaving an inheritance. Instead, the opposite was true.

How is this the case? Essentially, scenarios (2) and (3) provide a cushion against the dreaded sequence-of-return risk that is such a fundamental challenge to building a sustainable retirement plan. When home equity is used last, retirees are spending down their volatile investment portfolio earlier in retirement and are more exposed to locking in portfolio losses, more easily leading them on the path to depletion. Shifting some spending to home equity can reduce these pressures on the investment portfolio.

With option (2), if home equity is spent first, the financial portfolio is left alone in the interim, providing a better chance to grow so that by the time home equity is spent, retirees will be able to continue with a given spending amount in their retirement using what is likely to be a lower withdrawal rate from a now-larger portfolio. They quantify that the costs and interest paid on the reverse mortgage, while substantial, are less than the benefits the strategy provides to retirees and their beneficiaries in terms of maintaining more overall wealth.

And option (3) provides a more sophisticated technique to grapple with sequence-of-return risk by only spending from the reverse mortgage line of credit when the retiree is vulnerable to locking in portfolio losses: spend from the line of credit only after years in which the financial portfolio has declined.

Sacks and Sacks make clear that their point is not that all retirees should open a reverse mortgage, but that retirees who wish to remain in their homes for as long as possible should view it as more than a last-resort option. If retirees spend at a higher level that risks investment portfolio depletion and creates a possibility for also needing to generate cash flows from their home equity, there is indeed a better way to approach this task than using the home only as a last resort.

In a sign that the time had finally come for the idea of coordinated spending from a reverse mortgage, Harold Evensky, Shaun Pfeiffer, and John Salter of Texas Tech University followed suit with two articles—beginning with the August 2012 issue of the *Journal of Financial Planning*—also investigating the role of a standby line of credit. They independently came to very similar conclusions as the Sacks brothers.

Harold Evensky said that the motivation for their research came about when the home-equity lines of credit he had established as a source of liquidity for his clients kept getting canceled during the financial crisis in 2008. The HECM line of credit was guaranteed to be there even in times of market stress. Evensky et al. wrote, "Although reverse mortgages aren't for everyone, the reluctance to consider use of reverse mortgages in the distribution phase limits the flexibility of distribution strategies."

Their first article in 2012 investigated the use of a HECM Saver line of credit (which, you may recall, had lower costs but was later merged with the HECM Standard in September 2013) as a ready source of cash to be used as a risk-management tool for retirement distributions. The purpose of their research was aligned with that of Sacks and Sacks: to test portfolio sustainability using

Monte Carlo simulations when portfolio distributions are coordinated with a reverse mortgage.

With a similar objective in mind, Evensky and team developed a coordinated strategy to better approximate using the reverse mortgage when the portfolio was in jeopardy. Rather than drawing from the HECM line of credit after years of market downturns, they instead drew from the line of credit whenever the remaining portfolio balance fell below the value indicated by a separate wealth glide-path capital-needs calculation. They determined the amount of remaining wealth required for each year of retirement to keep the spending plan on a sustainable path through the desired planning horizon. After experimenting with this critical path for remaining wealth, they determined that drawing from the reverse mortgage worked best when remaining wealth fell to less than 80 percent of the wealth-glide path. This helped avoid overuse of the line of credit while still providing a mechanism to avoid selling financial assets at overly depreciated prices, thereby helping mitigate the sequence-of-return risk.

Another difference between their research and that of the Sacks brothers is that whenever remaining wealth grew enough to be back above the 80 percent barrier for their critical-path trajectory, Evensky and company worked to preserve a larger line of credit for future use by voluntarily paying back any outstanding loan balance throughout retirement. This contrasted with Sacks and Sacks, who made no voluntary repayments.

Evensky has heralded the value of using cash reserves as a buffer asset to mitigate sequence risk since the 1980s. Cash provides a drag on potential portfolio returns, but its presence serves as an alternative to financing spending by selling other assets at a loss. He suggested having two years of spending in a separate bucket and investing remaining funds with a total-return investment perspective. He viewed this as a compromise between the offsetting factors of the drag on returns created by holding more cash and not completely protecting the remaining portfolio if market declines last longer than two years.

The reverse mortgage research of these two articles follows along the same path, with the line of credit used as a buffer asset in place of a larger cash reserve. In the 2012 article, they replaced the two-year cash reserve with a six-month cash reserve, and they used the line of credit to refill the reserve, reduce the cash drag, and provide a source of funds not impacted by declining market returns.

Their glide-path approach to choosing when to tap the line of credit establishes rules that keep better track of cumulative outcomes, so it makes intuitive sense. However, in practical terms, calculating the wealth glide-path can be difficult, especially if taxes are incorporated into the analysis, so that a market downturn can also lower the tax bill and offset some capital needs. Their 2012 research uses the line of credit as a source of funds only when the portfolio is below the mark set by the glide path *and* the cash-reserve bucket has been depleted.

As with Sacks and Sacks, they found that using the standby line of credit improved portfolio survival without creating an adverse impact on median remaining wealth (including remaining home equity). This provided independent confirmation that the reverse mortgage line of credit can help mitigate sequence-of-return risk without impacting legacy goals. They also confirmed that having a larger line of credit (either through a higher PLF with lower interest rates or greater home value) relative to the portfolio size heightens the likelihood of sustaining a positive portfolio balance. Evensky and company conclude that a standby line of credit deserves a role in mainstream retirement income planning for four reasons:

1. It reduces the need to maintain a large cash buffer.

2. It provides flexibility to hold on to investments during bear markets.

3. It allows flexibility to use home equity as a source of spending.

4. It improves portfolio survivorship rates without adversely impacting legacy.

In December 2013, the same authors returned with a second study on using a standby line of credit for retirement income planning. This time, they shifted the focus to how much the sustainable withdrawal rate could be increased with a line of credit while maintaining a 90 percent success rate over a 30-year retirement. They confirmed that the standby line of credit helps sustain higher withdrawal rates when retirement starts in a low-interest-rate environment and/or the home is worth more relative to the investments.

Consistent with other withdrawal-rate research using lower capital-market expectations than the historical averages, they calculated that the sustainable spending rate without a reverse mortgage is 3.25 percent. With a reverse mortgage, the withdrawal rate can reach 6.5 percent. The higher number happens when the home value matches the portfolio value and interest rates are low at the start of retirement. They noted that these higher withdrawal rates are on par with those obtained through dynamic spending strategies that can involve substantial spending reductions over time, but the HECM strategy can sustain the higher spending rate without such reductions.

Bringing Tenure Payments to the Forefront

December 2013 was a busy month for research articles on reverse mortgages in the *Journal of Financial Planning.* Another contribution published that month was Gerald Wagner's "The 6.0 Percent Rule." Based on the title alone, it would seem to provide only further confirmation of the previous research, namely that strategic use of a line of credit can enhance sustainability for higher spending rates.

However, this article provides an important further detail to the research, earning its place in the apex of this first generation of research from 2012 and 2013. Wagner contributes the idea that when there is an upward-sloping yield curve for interest rates (interest rates for long-term bonds are higher than for short-term bonds, which is the normal situation), setting up term or tenure payments with a reverse mortgage is more effective than drawing down a line of credit in other ways. The tenure and term payments are based on a higher assumed interest rate for the 10-year Treasury (plus the same lender's margin and mortgage insurance premium as with line-of-credit growth), while the line of credit will grow at a rate based on the lower 1-month or 1-year Treasury rate as the variable component. If short-term interest rates do not rise rapidly, tenure and term payments can be larger than a sustainable distribution level from the line of credit.

Term and tenure payments provide a different view about the HECM principal limit. They offer fixed, ongoing payments for as long as the borrower remains in the home and eligible, or until the term finishes. A long life could lead to one being able to withdraw more than the principal limit, especially for tenure payments, as they continue even after the line of credit would have otherwise been exhausted. Term payments are calculated to avoid exhausting the principal limit, but an unexpected increase in interest rates could potentially cause the loan balance to exceed the principal limit. When this happens, full payments are guaranteed as well, for the length of the term and as long as the borrower remains eligible.

My reverse mortgage calculator allows users to determine the value of term and tenure payments from a reverse mortgage in addition to seeing the value of the line of credit that could be created.

An Updated Test of Portfolio Coordination Strategies

Further studies reaching similar conclusions arrived in subsequent years. But I think the previous discussion provides a sufficient glimpse at how these studies work and the results they provide. Let's jump to the present with a case study that provides a deeper look into different ways to incorporate a HECM into a retirement spending strategy. We will see how these pieces can fit together into an overall retirement plan.

In earlier editions of this book, I used the same type of Monte Carlo simulations as the previous research to test different strategies. Monte Carlo simulations generate randomized sequences of interest rates, housing prices, and investment returns to see how retirement strategies perform in different market environments. This approach provides a probability of success for meeting financial goals over time for different strategies and allows for examining the remaining household wealth. But I think that Monte Carlo simulations may not be entirely intuitive for readers who are not already familiar with these techniques. As such, to simplify these explanations and hopefully make the analysis more transparent, I have decided to switch the analysis here to using rolling historical periods from US data in the same manner that William Bengen used to create the conventional 4 percent rule for retirement spending.

Using historical data can be more intuitive as readers might more easily be able to imagine what it was like to retire in different historical environments, and to know that the underlying financial market data reflects situations that have happened, rather than being randomized sequences of possibilities.

An important point to highlight is that I am assuming that the case study happens in 2023, as I use the tax laws and HECM rules as they exist in early 2023. This includes the 2023 tax brackets that will adjust for inflation until 2026, and then revert to their 2017 levels (with inflation adjustments) as part of the provisions of the Tax Cuts and Jobs Act passed that year.

The purpose of using historical data is not to shift back in time, but rather to provide a range of possible experiences for stock returns, bond returns, interest rates, inflation, and home prices, from the perspective of considering if these historical market outcomes began anew in 2023. In other words, the simulated experience starting from 1950, for instance, just considers how a retiree in 2023 would fair with different strategies under current tax and HECM rules if the retiree subsequently experienced the sequence of market outcomes that begin in 1950, and so on. I think it is important to highlight this, as otherwise some readers may be confused, noting that HECMs did not even exist in 1950.

We consider a case study for a couple who recently retired after both celebrated their 62nd birthdays in January 2023. For their retirement finances, their priority is to build a financial plan that will cover their spending goals through age 95. In cases where this is feasible, a secondary priority is to maximize the after-tax surplus of wealth for their beneficiaries.

They have $900,000 in investment assets. These retirement assets include $290,000 in a taxable brokerage account (with a $130,000 cost basis), $510,000 in a tax-deferred Individual Retirement Account (IRA), and $100,000 in a tax-free Roth IRA.

They also own a home appraised at $450,000 with no outstanding mortgage debt. If not apparent, I designed the case study with investment assets that are double the home value. As noted in the discussion of past research, the outcomes for using a HECM are strengthened as the home value increases in size relative to the investment portfolio.

This is a one-earner couple, and the primary insurance amount for the worker's Social Security retirement benefit is $2,500 per month. Annually, when claiming at full retirement age and with the spousal benefit included, Social Security will provide $45,000 of inflation-adjusted lifetime income (in age 62 dollars), starting at age 67.

For the HECM, I assume that they pay full upfront costs without any lender credits to avoid providing any advantage to HECM strategies. This includes an origination fee of $6,000, a 2 percent initial mortgage insurance premium of $9,000, and other closing costs of $4,000. This is a combined total cost of $19,000 when the loan is initiated. These costs are financed in the loan balance. I also assume a lender's margin of 2.5 percent for the HECM.

For the last-resort strategy, which opens a reverse mortgage later in retirement, I assume the other closing costs grow with the consumer price index until this time, and the mortgage insurance premium is 2 percent of the subsequent home value (or the maximum lending limit, which I also assume grows with inflation). I keep the origination fees fixed under the current schedule as they are not automatically adjusted for inflation. This provides a benefit to last-resort strategies, since it is likely that at some point HUD will increase the origination fee schedule to help them keep pace with inflation.

The initial principal limit for the loan will vary over time in the historical data, as the expected rate to determine this value will include the 10-year Treasury rate at the start of each retirement simulation. The subsequent principal limit growth is determined by the sum of the 2.5 percent lender margin, the ongoing 0.5 percent mortgage insurance, and the variable rate of interest offered by the current 1-year Treasury rate.

As for the couple's retirement liabilities, their projected retirement expenses and home property taxes equal an inflation-adjusted $67,000. They will also seek to spend an additional $10,000 each year through age 74 that is not inflation-adjusted, to get the most enjoyment out of their go-go retirement years. They live in a state with no income tax, but they will need to pay federal income taxes—an additional expense that will be included in this analysis beyond these mentioned spending goals.

I calculate taxes on their portfolio distributions, including qualified dividends, interest, and long-term capital gains from their taxable account, the ordinary income generated from IRA distributions, and the precise amount of taxes due on their Social Security benefits. I also calculate any Medicare premium surcharges if their modified adjusted gross income exceeds the relevant thresholds, as well as any potential net investment income surtaxes due. These taxes are calculated based on tax law in early 2023, including the shift to higher tax rates in 2026 that is part of current law. Tax brackets increase with inflation, though the thresholds for determining taxes on Social Security are not inflation adjusted.

Their investment assets are all held in a balanced fund with a 60 percent stock allocation representing large-capitalization US stocks and a 40 percent allocation to 10-year Constant Maturity Treasuries. Stock dividends are assumed to be qualified and receive preferential income tax rates, bond interest is taxed as ordinary income, and I assume that unsold investments do not generate any unrealized capital gains distributions.

For investment distributions needed to cover retirement spending, the approach used is to first take any required minimum distributions from the tax-deferred account, which begin at age 72. If this, plus Social Security benefits and any distributions from the HECM, is less than the desired spending and federal income taxes due, additional withdrawals are then taken from the taxable account first, until empty, then the tax-deferred account, and lastly the tax-free Roth account. Distributions are taken at the start of each year.

Reverse Mortgages and Asset Allocation

I assume that the couple keeps the same asset allocation with or without the reverse mortgage. It is worth commenting that a reverse mortgage can increase risk capacity and reduce risk exposure for the household, which could justify a higher stock allocation than otherwise, if they are comfortable with it. The HECM line of credit provides a source of liquid reserve assets to manage spending shocks so that the portfolio is less exposed to a surprise distribution need. It can also help to manage market volatility by reducing pressure on making portfolio distributions. Both factors can justify using a higher stock allocation.

This distribution strategy is directionally correct in terms of providing tax efficiency for retirement spending, though a more blended strategy that mixes taxable and tax-deferred distributions at first, and then tax-deferred and tax-free distributions later, to provide control over the adjusted gross income, could work better. I explore this more sophisticated approach in Chapter 7 when I look at how a HECM might help contribute to a strategic Roth conversion strategy. If Social Security, HECM distributions, and required minimum distributions from the IRA exceed the desired spending level and taxes due in any year, then any surplus is added as new savings to the taxable account.

Tax Planning for Efficient Retirement Distributions

This discussion about income taxes due when funding a retirement spending goal assumes that the reader has familiarity with tax-planning concepts for retirement income. This includes understanding how federal income taxes are calculated in terms of ordinary income, preferential income sources, the taxation of Social Security benefits, and income-related adjustments for Medicare premiums. Readers seeking more background on these topics may consult my *Retirement Planning Guidebook: Navigating the Important Decisions for Retirement Success*.

The legacy value of assets reflects the after-tax value of investments and housing wealth left over. Taxable assets receive a step-up in basis at death, providing their full value for heirs. For tax-deferred assets, I assume that adult children will be beneficiaries, and the SECURE Act requires them to spend down the account within a 10-year window when they may still be in their peak earnings years and face higher tax rates. To reflect this, I assume that remaining tax-deferred assets will be taxed at a 25 percent rate to reduce their legacy value to heirs. Tax-free Roth assets also face the same distribution requirements, but they will not be taxable to heirs, so their full value passes as legacy.

The house also receives a step-up in basis, and net housing wealth available as a legacy reflects 95 percent of the home's appraised value, less the loan balance due on a HECM. The 95 percent is used to determine whether the non-recourse provision applies and, otherwise, this could be viewed as a selling cost for heirs to create liquidity for the housing asset received. As a non-recourse loan, the legacy value of the house is $0 if the loan balance is greater than 95 percent of the home's appraised value.

When the HECM is opened at the start of retirement, it can create situations in which the available line of credit remains despite a stagnating home value, causing the principal limit for the loan to be greater than what the home is worth. In this case, HECM distributions can be supported without a negative legacy impact. This could also happen with the last-resort strategy, though it is less likely with the shorter horizon for the principal limit of the HECM to grow, when the loan initiation is delayed.

If the entire spending goal cannot be met over the retirement planning horizon, I calculate the spending shortfall as a negative legacy, reflecting the amount of desired spending that cannot be met. It is the sum of desired spending less the available income sources. Shortfalls only happen when the investment assets and the HECM line of credit are fully depleted (or in the case of tenure payments, when the investment assets are depleted).

When the HECM is opened at the start of retirement, any shortfalls will likely happen only when and if the loan balance exceeds the home value. But that is not always the case. With the last-resort strategy, it would be more common for the line of credit to be depleted despite there still being some remaining housing wealth, if the home value is greater than the HECM loan balance. In these scenarios, a retiree could downsize the home or otherwise cut spending. But to avoid confusion, I treat the retirement as a "failure" in the sense that the spending goals cannot be fully met and the remaining housing wealth cannot be tapped without more drastic action. I do not offset the calculated shortfall by the amount of the inaccessible housing wealth. Nonetheless, with the conservative spending goal chosen for the case study that offers a high success rate, the number of cases where this issue is relevant is quite limited.

To analyze these retirement strategies, I use financial market and housing data that is freely available from Robert Shiller's website. His housing data extends back to 1890, which is the constraint that allows us to consider all the relevant data ranging from 1890 to 2022. The historical performance is summarized in Exhibit 5.1. Stocks are represented with large-capitalization US stocks that eventually became the S&P 500. Since 1890, they averaged 10.8 percent returns, with a compounded growth rate over time (geometric mean) of 9.2 percent and volatility of 18.1 percent. The dividend yield on stocks averaged 4.1 percent historically.

Exhibit 5.1
Summary Statistics of U.S. Returns and Inflation Data, 1890-2022

	Arithmetic Means	Geometric Means	Standard Deviations
Large-Cap US Stocks (Total Returns)	10.8%	9.2%	18.1%
Large-Cap US Stocks (Dividend Yield)	4.1%	—	1.6%
10-Year Treasury Bonds (Total Returns)	4.6%	4.4%	6.8%
10-Year Treasury Bonds (Bond Yields)	4.5%	—	2.4%
1-Year Treasury Bills	4.3%	4.2%	3.0%
Home Prices (Case-Shiller Index)	3.7%	3.5%	7.3%
Inflation (Consumer Price Index)	2.9%	2.8%	5.2%

Source: Robert Shiller's website (www.econ.yale.edu/~shiller/data.htm)

Bonds are represented with 10-year Constant Maturity Treasury bonds, and these bond yields are also used for calculating the expected rate and the tenure payment for the HECM. These bonds average 4.6 percent returns historically, with a 6.8 percent volatility. Treasury bills with a 1-year Constant Maturity are also included, not as an investment asset but as the variable rate used to calculate principal limit growth with the HECM. Historically, bills averaged 4.3 percent. For Treasury bills only, Shiller is the source through 2009, and the Federal Reserve is the source for the most recent years.

For housing prices, I use the Case-Shiller national index of home prices. Individual home prices will be more volatile, but I do not adjust for this, assuming instead that the couple's home value marches in line with the aggregate index. It is also important to note that many retirees may live in less trendy neighborhoods as they age, and their homes may not appreciate as fast as the national average. The Case-Shiller index grew at an average rate of 3.7 percent with a 7.3 percent volatility. This is only 0.8 percent more, on average, than the 2.9 percent growth rate for the Consumer Price Index. While recent years may have created the impression that single family homes are a rapidly appreciating asset, we must note that since 1890, home price growth has fallen behind that of both Treasury bonds and bills, while also experiencing greater volatility than these asset classes.

We will investigate four retirement spending strategies that use the investment portfolio and home equity in different ways:

1. *Home equity as last resort.* This strategy represents the conventional wisdom regarding home equity. It is the only home-equity strategy that delays opening a line of credit with a reverse mortgage. The investment portfolio is spent first. If the portfolio depletes at some point, a HECM line of credit is opened at that time. Spending needs are then met with the line of credit until it is fully used as well. The PLF is calculated using the current PLF table, for the updated age and interest rate at the future date, when the investments deplete, assuming the same 2.5 percent lender's margin rate. Retirement shortfalls begin once the line of credit is fully used.

2. *Use tenure payment.* This strategy uses the tenure-payment option on the net value of the principal limit after financing the upfront costs. With an initial home value of $450,000, an age 62 start, $19,000 of financed upfront costs, and a 2.5 percent lender's margin, annual tenure payments will range in value as based on the 10-year Treasury rate at the start of each retirement.

A higher interest rate will increase the tenure payment as a percentage of the principal limit, but it also causes the initial principal limit to be smaller. As shown in Exhibit 5.2, the peak tenure payment can be achieved at a 3.25 percent expected rate, when the annual income provided by the tenure payment is $10,624. This could be accomplished with a 10-year Treasury rate of 0.75 percent, leading to a PLF of 52.2 percent. If the Treasury rate were 5 percent, for instance, the PLF would only be 30.7 percent; though the tenure payment would be a higher percentage of this value, it is still less overall. Higher interest rates simply cause too much of a reduction to the initial principal limit factor for the tenure payment to increase.

Exhibit 5.2
The Relationship between Expected Rates and Tenure Payments,
$450,000 Home Value, 62-Year-Old Borrower

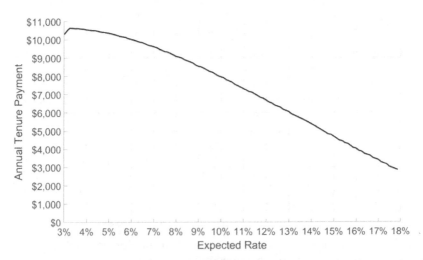

The spending supported through the HECM tenure payment does not adjust for inflation. The remainder of spending needs are covered by the investment portfolio for as long as financial assets remain. As the tenure payments help offset some of the need for portfolio distributions, the tenure payment helps to manage sequence-of-return risk by reducing the portfolio withdrawal rate and, thus, its vulnerability to a market downturn.

3. *Portfolio coordination strategy.* This strategy opens the line of credit at the start of retirement and draws from it, when credit remains, for any year in which the nominal balance of the investment portfolio at the start of the year

fell below its $900,000 combined level at the start of retirement. Since the HECM distribution is not taxable income, I decided to only draw 50 percent of the portfolio spending need from the HECM, before calculating any additional taxes on the distributions to cover the other 50 percent, instead of using the HECM for the full amount. This avoids wasting capacity to pay taxes at low rates, which is especially important in the first 5 years of the case study, before Social Security begins. With a full HECM draw there would be no taxable income to even benefit from the standard deduction. The rest of the spending need, and any taxes it generates, is taken from investments when available. In years that the portfolio balance exceeds the initial $900,000 threshold, the reverse mortgage is not used, and the entire spending need is covered through portfolio distributions. No effort is made to repay the loan balance until the full loan becomes due.

Decision Rules for Portfolio Coordination Strategies

Separate from working on this book, I compared multiple decision rules about when to draw from a buffer asset, such as a HECM, when coordinating spending from an investment portfolio. The rules I compared included the Sacks and Sacks approach that based the decision on portfolio performance in the preceding year, and the Evensky, Pfeiffer, and Salter approach, which based the decision on a capital-needs analysis for the remaining portfolio wealth needed each year to sustain the spending strategy. I found that the rule I selected for use in this book works just as well as any of the more sophisticated methods I tested. Just as importantly, this rule is simple for retirees to use in practice. One only compares the current value of the investment assets with the nominal value at the start of retirement to make the decision about which asset to use for the current year spending.

---

4. *Portfolio coordination strategy with voluntary repayments.* This strategy follows the same procedure for opening and spending from the line of credit as in the previous strategy. The difference is a provision to voluntarily pay down the loan balance if the portfolio recovers sufficiently. In years that the total investment assets exceed 125 percent of the initial investment value ($1.125 million), and in which the loan balance is less than 75 percent of the home's appraised value at that time, the loan balance is paid down until investments either reach the 125 percent threshold or the remaining loan balance is just $100. A nominal loan balance is needed to keep the credit line open. The reason for only paying down the loan balance when it is sufficiently smaller than the home's value is to take advantage of any non-recourse opportunities for the loan, if it looks like the loan balance is on track to exceed what the home is worth.

Shifting to results, to understand how different HECM strategies can support a retirement plan, I provide an overview of results for this case study in Exhibit 5.3. This compares the "conventional wisdom" last-resort strategy with three strategies that open the HECM at the start of retirement and use it more systematically throughout. The four strategies are all comparable, because they all allow home equity to be used to meet spending goals alongside the investment portfolio. What differs among the strategies are the decisions about when to spend from the portfolio and when from the home.

Of the 100 rolling historical periods available for this analysis, we find that the last resort strategy supports the largest net legacy at age 95 in 18 percent of cases, compared to the tenure payment strategy that comes out on top 66 percent of the time, the portfolio coordination strategy winning 7 percent of the time, and the coordinated strategy with voluntary repayments winning 9 percent of the time. The last resort strategy supports the least legacy in 39 percent of cases.

This case study shows with historical simulations that the last-resort option is the least effective way to coordinate the portfolio with a reverse mortgage for meeting retirement spending goals. It generally only comes out ahead by avoiding the need to pay upfront costs to set up the reverse mortgage, in scenarios in which the investment portfolio performs well enough that home equity is not needed to meet spending goals, and in other occasional situations where the overall mix of market returns, interest rate changes, and home appreciation leaves it in a slightly better position.

Exhibit 5.3
Comparing Net Legacy Wealth for Various HECM Strategies

		HECM as Last Resort	Tenure Payment	Portfolio Coordination Strategy	Portfolio Coordination Strategy with Voluntary Repayments
Ranking the Strategies	First	18%	66%	7%	9%
	Second	26%	12%	49%	13%
	Third	17%	11%	29%	43%
	Fourth	39%	11%	15%	35%
Legacy Wealth Percentile	Best Case	$4,787,592	$4,599,979	$4,328,866	$4,636,410
	90%	$3,144,565	$3,417,101	$3,188,639	$3,063,826
	75%	$1,924,360	$2,115,011	$2,053,457	$1,911,647
	50%	$958,030	$1,125,711	$1,026,933	$1,045,334
	25%	$605,529	$764,875	$675,156	$655,157
	10%	$328,093	$538,395	$455,797	$422,811
	Worst Case	-$140,817	$151,520	$2,488	$2,488
Success Rate for Covering all Spending		95.0%	100.0%	100.0%	100.0%

We will explore more about what triggers these different outcomes, but first we can look at the distribution of legacy wealth across the historical outcomes for each strategy. In the best historical outcome, the last-resort strategy supports the largest net legacy. This is a retirement starting with the market returns from 1982, on which I will comment further below. Aside from this "best" case, for much of the distribution the tenure payment strategy supports the largest net legacy as its ability to reduce the distribution needs from investments allows the investments to grow at a rate that could more than offset the costs of the reverse mortgage. We also see from the exhibit that the last-resort strategy avoided shortfalls in 95 percent of the historical scenarios, and the other three HECM uses could all avoid shortfalls in 100 percent of these historical cases.

Exhibit 5.4 provides more details on when the last-resort option is used in this case study. In funding the couple's spending needs, investment assets deplete in 14 of the 100 simulated retirements. The exhibit shows these years, as well as the age that investments deplete and the HECM is initiated, to continue the retirement spending. In 5 of the 100 cases (a 5 percent failure rate), the HECM line of credit is also subsequently fully depleted, leading to an inability to continue meeting the overall spending goal. This happens for the retirements beginning in 1965-66, 1968-69, and 1973, and at ages ranging from 89 to 95.

Exhibit 5.4
Making Use of the Last-Resort Option –Planning Through Age 95

Retirement Year	Age HECM is Initiated as Last Resort	Age That Spending Goal Can No Longer Be Fully Met
1906	89	
1912	94	
1916	90	
1937	89	
1962	93	
1964	90	
1965	85	95
1966	82	89
1967	86	
1968	84	95
1969	84	93
1971	95	
1972	86	
1973	81	89

Continuing with this analysis of the last-resort strategy, Exhibit 5.5 shows the net legacy wealth with this approach, using the market returns and home appreciation starting from 1890 through 1989 (and ending in 1923 through 2022). Net legacy wealth is circled for years that the last resort was triggered (as seen in the previous exhibit), and we do observe the shortfalls for the 5 retirement years in the 1960s and 1973. Meanwhile, legacies were the highest for retirements starting in 1921 and 1982. The median legacy at age 95 in inflation-adjusted terms from the start of retirement was $958,030.

Exhibit 5.5
Net Real Legacy Wealth, HECM as a Last-Resort Strategy

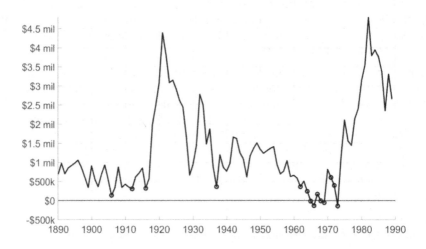

This best-case scenario, in terms of supporting the highest net legacy at age 95, created by the market returns from 1982 to 2015, deserves further comment. As we compare different strategies using HECMs, we will repeatedly see 1982 as a rare case in which it is hard to beat the last-resort conventional wisdom. Exhibit 5.6 helps to highlight why this is the case. It shows the compounded returns over the first 10 years of retirement from each historical starting point and the historical 10-year Treasury bond yield at the retirement start. In 1982, the compounded return from the investment portfolio over the subsequent 10 years was 16.3 percent. This is the opposite of sequence-of-return risk. Experiencing such a wonderful return at the start of retirement sets the course for either very high sustainable spending or a greater legacy with a given spending goal.

Also, 1982 is the year with the highest 10-year Treasury rate, which was 14.6 percent. HECMs work better when interest rates are low, because this allows for a greater principal limit and more borrowing capacity. In 1982, the HECM is not able to offer much to the retiree. At this interest rate, the principal limit factor is 8.6 percent, and the initial principal limit is only $38,700 on the $450,000 home. After financing the upfront costs, that only leaves a net principal limit of $19,700, which is not much to work with. While we will find that strategic use of the HECM will generally improve outcomes for the retirement plan, 1982 presents a glaring exception.

Exhibit 5.6
Portfolio Returns and Bond Yields

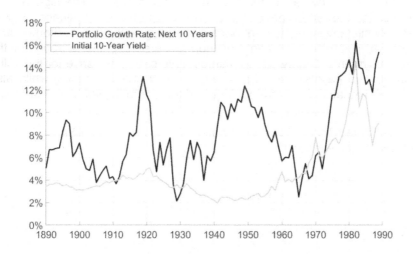

Exhibit 5.7
Comparing the Tenure Payment Strategy to the Last-Resort Strategy
Net Real Legacy Wealth (Tenure Payments - Last Resort)

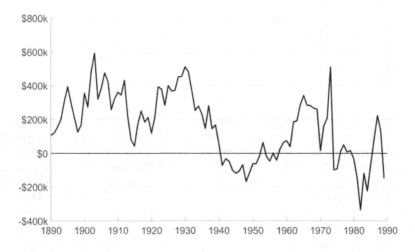

For specific strategies, we next compare the tenure payment strategy to the last-resort strategy. Exhibit 5.7 shows the after-tax real value of remaining assets at age 95 for tenure payments, less the value for the last resort. It is the difference in final legacy. When these values are larger than $0, which happens 76 percent of the time, the tenure payment provides a better outcome, and vice versa. The tenure payment strategy does fall behind in the 1940s and early 1980s. In the 1940s, I cannot identify a particular reason for why this happens, as there are so many intertwined aspects at work between changing interest rates, investment performance, and home value growth. In the early 1980s, the reason is understandable. The high interest rates cause the tenure payments to be low and the loan balance to grow faster, while investments are otherwise doing well. Strong home price appreciation is also preventing the non-recourse aspects to apply for the tenure payments. Otherwise, we can observe strong evidence for the value of the tenure payment strategy to support retirement spending while also laying a foundation for larger net legacies relative to the last-resort strategy.

Exhibit 5.8
Comparing the Tenure Payment Strategy to the Last-Resort Strategy
Net Real Legacy Wealth

The differences in net legacies shown in Exhibit 5.7 provide a straightforward way to view the results, but this obscures one detail. Does the tenure payment help to manage retirement risk? Does it outperform at times when net legacies are otherwise low or high? Exhibit 5.8 helps to remedy this detail by plotting the net real legacy with the last-resort strategy against the net real legacy with the tenure payment. If the dot is above the diagonal line, then the net legacy is larger with tenure payments, and vice versa. I have circled the outcomes in this exhibit, which help clarify the risk management principles. The tenure payment option consistently provides a larger net legacy when asset values are otherwise low and the retirement is more at risk. Risk-averse retirees will want to pay more attention to the circled outcomes. Placed into context, the point farthest to the right is 1982, when the last-resort approach supported a net legacy of $4.78 million. In that case, the net legacy with the tenure payment was $4.45 million, which is still quite reasonable and does not place the retirement at risk. We tend to care less about outcomes in which both strategies support larger legacies, and want more emphasis on obtaining protection in outcomes where retirements are at greater risk. The tenure payment option fulfills this purpose.

Next, Exhibit 5.9 makes this same comparison for the portfolio coordination strategy and the last-resort strategy. The difference in net legacy wealth is greater than $0 in 56 percent of these cases, which reflects the historical frequency for the portfolio coordination strategy to provide a better retirement outcome than the last-resort strategy. On average, the portfolio coordination strategy supported a $67,140 increase in net real legacy. The last-resort strategy enjoyed the best relative outperformance in 1982, but this was simply because portfolio growth was so strong throughout retirement that the portfolio coordination strategy never needed to be used, and the upfront setup cost for the reverse mortgage was unnecessary. The exhibit does provide evidence that retirees can expect that they will typically be better off with the portfolio coordination strategy than with leaving the HECM as a last resort.

Exhibit 5.9
Comparing the Portfolio Coordination Strategy to the Last-Resort Strategy
Net Real Legacy Wealth (Portfolio Coordination - Last Resort)

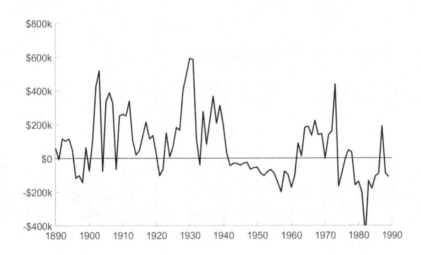

Exhibit 5.10 provides the same comparison for the portfolio coordination strategy with voluntary repayments on the loan balance against the last-resort strategy. The story is similar. Though the portfolio coordination strategy here only provides a larger net legacy than the last-resort strategy in 45 percent of the cases, the differences tend to be larger when the portfolio coordination works. On average, net legacies were $30,303 larger with portfolio coordination. Readers may conclude, at least for this case study, that voluntary repayments on the loan balance are not necessary.

Exhibit 5.10
Comparing Portfolio Coordination with Repayment to Last-Resort Strategy
Net Real Legacy Wealth (Portfolio Coord. with Repayment - Last Resort)

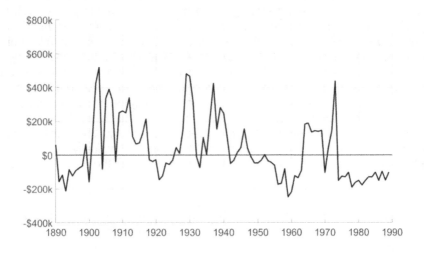

To provide a deeper sense about the mechanics for how these strategies perform, I will also show results on a year-by-year basis for the retirement period lasting from 1962 to 1995. These numbers are shown in nominal terms, rather than real inflation-adjusted terms, to make it easier to follow the changes. Please note this difference, as the preceding exhibits showed net legacy wealth in real terms leading to smaller numbers that reflect purchasing power for the start of those retirements. With these year-by-year exhibits, the net legacy values can be understood in 1995 dollars instead of in 1962 dollars, as the previous exhibits showed.

I pick 1962 as a representative year when the last-resort option is used but the retirement is still a success. As noted, a last-resort HECM is needed in only 14 of the historical cases, of which nine succeeded in continuing all spending through age 95. Exhibit 5.11 provides the details for the last-resort strategy. To fund the spending goal and pay income taxes, the taxable account depletes in 1966, the tax-deferred account depletes in 1984, and the Roth account depletes in 1993, when the couple is 93 years old.

They initiate a reverse mortgage at the start of 1993, providing an initial principal limit of $1,308,711 on a home that was worth $2,209,180 at the start of the year (which is the value of the home at the end of the previous year). The exhibit shows the 1993 principal limit as larger because it is the end-of-year value. With inflation growth, the maximum lending limit grew to $4.8 million. They use the last-resort strategy to successfully support their retirement through age 95, with an additional line of credit still available at the end of 1995. At the end, their home is worth $2,335,483, and the loan balance is $409,463. Their net housing wealth, which is 95 percent of the appraised home value less the loan balance due, is **$1,809,246**. As they do not have investment assets, this is the legacy available to heirs, who would need to sell the home to repay the loan balance or otherwise refinance or pay off the balance, if they wish to keep the home.

Next, Exhibit 5.12 provides the scenario in which they use the tenure payment option. The annual tenure payments total $9,920, which helps to reduce pressure on the investment portfolio to support the retirement spending need. The taxable account depletes in 1966, but the tax-deferred account and Roth account are both still going strong in 1995. The IRA has $930,367, which translates to $697,775 after the assumed 25 percent tax rate is applied to beneficiaries. The Roth IRA provides $2,039,688 income-tax free for beneficiaries. The Roth IRA alone is worth more than the net legacy provided with the last-resort strategy. The tenure payment reduces the need for portfolio distributions, creating that synergistic impact described in Chapter 1 (Exhibit 1.6), which allows for greater long-term portfolio growth. Small changes in portfolio distribution rates have large impacts on subsequent portfolio values.

Meanwhile, at age 95, the HECM balance stands at $3,013,983. This is larger than the home value, but the tenure payments are protected and the non-recourse aspect of the loan means that net housing wealth is $0. The total net legacy for this strategy is **$2,737,463**. This is $928,216 more, in 1995 dollars, available for heirs than could be provided by using the HECM as a last resort. The composition of the wealth has changed, as now legacy is provided in terms of retirement accounts with simple beneficiary designations, and the home can be turned over with a deed in lieu of foreclosure. If the heirs wish to keep the home, they can pay 95 percent of the appraised value ($2,218,709) and have an additional $518,754 left over.

Exhibit 5.13 provides the results when using the portfolio coordination strategy with the HECM. In this scenario, the remaining investment balance has fallen below the initial $900,000 starting level by the end of the first year. HECM distributions begin in 1963 and continue with 8 different distributions over the subsequent years as the portfolio balance continues to fluctuate. With this coordination, the portfolio balance does not dip below its initial level again after 1978.

At the end of 1978, investment assets total $922,384, and the portfolio distribution in 1979 represents 6.21 percent of remaining assets. With the last-resort strategy, the withdrawal rate from remaining investments needed to meet 1979's spending and taxes is 10.18 percent. By drawing strategically from the HECM, the portfolio coordination strategy also helped reduce taxes during most of these precarious retirement years. The HECM spending helped get the investment portfolio back on track. With the coordination strategy, the IRA still holds $284,501 at the end of retirement, and the Roth IRA holds $2,039,688. The loan balance exceeds the home value, so there is no net housing wealth, but the overall legacy after accounting for income taxes to the beneficiary on the IRA is **$2,253,064**. This is $443,817 more than the last-resort strategy, in 1995 dollars. This is the synergistic aspect of the coordinated strategy at work, as it protected the portfolio in pivotal retirement years, achieving gains that more than compensated for the HECM costs.

There is one further point we can make about this strategy, which I did not count as part of net legacy and is more controversial. At the end of age 94 (I'll use this, since I assume the couple passed away at the end of age 95), the principal limit is $3.06 million, the HECM balance is $2.8 million, and the home value is $2.28 million. There is still $253,816 left in the line of credit, while the loan is already underwater. If they wish to engage in the "ruthless option," which involves taking a windfall from the line of credit while the non-recourse aspect of the loan already applies, such that the mortgage insurance fund is required to make up the difference, they could simply withdraw the additional amount from the line of credit and invest it in the taxable account to further increase the net legacy value of assets.

Finally, Exhibit 5.14 provides results for the portfolio coordination strategy with voluntary repayments. It begins in the same manner as the preceding portfolio coordination strategy, with identical outcomes through the end of 1983. At the end of 1983, the total investment balance had recovered to be $35,484 more than the 125 percent threshold used to support voluntary repayments, and the loan balance was still well below the home value. Voluntary repayments happen for four years (1984-1987). This reduces the loan balance and increases the credit line. These voluntary repayments deplete the investment assets faster, as only the Roth IRA has assets at the end of 1995. Its balance is $1,133,408. With the voluntary repayments, net housing wealth is $3,023 at the end of life, after the beneficiaries sell the home and pay off the loan balance. The total net legacy is **$1,136,431**, which is $672,815 less than the last-resort strategy. In hindsight, voluntary repayment did not help because strong portfolio growth means they did not need the line of credit and funds would have been better off in the investment portfolio. As mentioned with the previous strategy, a ruthless option does also exist here, which could provide a windfall of funds to push net legacy higher. At age 94, the line of credit is $1,032,649, while the net housing wealth is $257,726.

With these four exhibits, we were able to track the specific year-by-year situation for the four reverse mortgage strategies with the 1962-1995 financial market data. For this period, and not counting use of the ruthless option, the tenure payment strategy provided the largest net legacy, followed by the portfolio coordination strategy, the last-resort strategy, and the coordination strategy with voluntary repayments.

I hope that being able to observe these year-by-year patterns can help readers better understand why and how these reverse mortgage strategies work, as the outcomes are no longer obscured by the lack of transparency created with Monte Carlo simulations that focus on the aggregate probability of success. While reverse mortgages can look expensive in isolation, they serve as a piece in a larger puzzle in which their costs can be offset by gains elsewhere in the overall financial plan, leading to better retirement outcomes. This can be seen consistently when applying historical market data to a case study based on current HECM rules and tax laws.

Reverse mortgages can help manage sequence risk for retirees by strategically and synergistically helping to preserve the investment portfolio throughout retirement. Gains created for investments will quite frequently exceed the costs of the reverse mortgage for a better overall outcome. Strategic spending from the reverse mortgage throughout retirement can help manage sequence-of-return risk by reducing the need for portfolio distributions at inopportune times, or by more generally reducing the need for portfolio distributions through the tenure payment. These synergies are what helps make the HECM an important tool for retirees.

Exhibit 5.11
Retirement Plan with Last Resort Strategy for HECM
Case Study for Market Data, 1962-1995

Year	Expenses and Taxes			Income Sources			Account Distributions		
	Pre-Tax Expenses	Income Taxes	Total Expenses	Total Income	Social Security	HECM Distribution	Taxable	Tax-Deferred	Tax Exempt
1962	$77,000	$0	$77,000	$77,000	$0	$0	$77,000	$0	$0
1963	$77,893	$0	$77,893	$77,893	$0	$0	$77,893	$0	$0
1964	$79,010	$0	$79,010	$79,010	$0	$0	$79,010	$0	$0
1965	$79,680	$0	$79,680	$79,680	$0	$0	$79,680	$0	$0
1966	$81,020	$7,739	$88,759	$88,759	$0	$0	$4,427	$84,333	$0
1967	$83,477	$3,911	$87,388	$87,388	$49,350	$0	$0	$38,038	$0
1968	$86,157	$4,152	$90,308	$90,308	$51,150	$0	$0	$39,158	$0
1969	$89,507	$4,452	$93,959	$93,959	$53,400	$0	$0	$40,559	$0
1970	$94,420	$4,893	$99,313	$99,313	$56,700	$0	$0	$42,613	$0
1971	$98,887	$5,293	$104,180	$104,180	$59,700	$0	$0	$44,480	$0
1972	$101,790	$5,554	$107,344	$107,343	$61,650	$0	$0	$45,693	$0
1973	$105,140	$5,854	$110,994	$110,994	$63,900	$0	$0	$47,094	$0
1974	$114,073	$6,655	$120,729	$120,728	$69,900	$0	$0	$50,828	$0
1975	$116,357	$3,916	$120,273	$120,272	$78,150	$0	$0	$42,122	$0
1976	$124,173	$4,617	$128,790	$128,790	$83,400	$0	$0	$45,390	$0
1977	$130,650	$5,198	$135,848	$135,848	$87,750	$0	$0	$48,098	$0
1978	$139,583	$5,999	$145,582	$145,582	$93,750	$0	$0	$51,832	$0
1979	$152,537	$7,161	$159,697	$159,697	$102,450	$0	$0	$57,247	$0
1980	$173,753	$9,063	$182,817	$182,816	$116,700	$0	$0	$66,116	$0
1981	$194,300	$10,906	$205,206	$205,206	$130,500	$0	$0	$74,706	$0
1982	$210,603	$12,368	$222,971	$222,971	$141,450	$0	$0	$81,521	$0
1983	$218,420	$13,069	$231,489	$231,489	$146,700	$0	$0	$84,789	$0
1984	$227,577	$5,670	$233,247	$233,247	$152,850	$0	$0	$55,745	$24,651
1985	$235,617	$0	$235,617	$235,617	$158,250	$0	$0	$0	$77,367
1986	$244,773	$0	$244,773	$244,773	$164,400	$0	$0	$0	$80,373
1987	$248,347	$0	$248,347	$248,347	$166,800	$0	$0	$0	$81,547
1988	$258,397	$0	$258,397	$258,397	$173,550	$0	$0	$0	$84,847
1989	$270,457	$0	$270,457	$270,457	$181,650	$0	$0	$0	$88,807
1990	$284,527	$0	$284,527	$284,527	$191,100	$0	$0	$0	$93,427
1991	$300,607	$0	$300,607	$300,607	$201,900	$0	$0	$0	$98,707
1992	$308,423	$0	$308,423	$308,423	$207,150	$0	$0	$0	$101,273
1993	$318,473	$0	$318,473	$318,473	$213,900	$8,783	$0	$0	$95,791
1994	$326,513	$0	$326,513	$326,513	$219,300	$107,213	$0	$0	$0
1995	$335,670	$0	$335,670	$335,670	$225,450	$110,220	$0	$0	$0

Exhibit 5.11 continued…

Remaining Investment Wealth			Housing Wealth				
Taxable	Tax-Deferred	Tax Exempt	Principal Limit	HECM Balance	Home Value	Net Housing Wealth	Net Legacy
$214,626	$513,893	$100,763	$0	$0	$450,000	$427,500	$1,128,309
$154,465	$580,539	$113,831	$0	$0	$451,450	$428,878	$1,132,578
$83,810	$644,817	$126,435	$0	$0	$460,634	$437,602	$1,131,459
$4,427	$691,199	$135,529	$0	$0	$469,334	$445,867	$1,104,223
$0	$595,064	$132,893	$0	$0	$475,618	$451,837	$1,031,028
$0	$604,709	$144,270	$0	$0	$479,968	$455,969	$1,053,771
$0	$605,138	$154,368	$0	$0	$490,602	$466,071	$1,074,293
$0	$523,011	$143,002	$0	$0	$513,802	$488,112	$1,023,373
$0	$537,315	$159,945	$0	$0	$552,470	$524,847	$1,087,778
$0	$550,182	$178,556	$0	$0	$593,555	$563,878	$1,155,071
$0	$562,372	$199,043	$0	$0	$619,173	$588,214	$1,209,037
$0	$471,176	$182,007	$0	$0	$634,157	$602,449	$1,137,838
$0	$373,637	$161,782	$0	$0	$662,675	$629,541	$1,071,550
$0	$416,017	$203,020	$0	$0	$737,395	$700,525	$1,215,558
$0	$412,239	$225,814	$0	$0	$776,208	$737,398	$1,272,392
$0	$347,995	$215,801	$0	$0	$842,833	$800,692	$1,277,489
$0	$325,270	$237,011	$0	$0	$967,853	$919,460	$1,400,424
$0	$293,674	$259,693	$0	$0	$1,123,602	$1,067,422	$1,547,372
$0	$263,028	$300,172	$0	$0	$1,267,766	$1,204,378	$1,701,821
$0	$182,145	$290,327	$0	$0	$1,358,905	$1,290,959	$1,717,896
$0	$133,905	$386,352	$0	$0	$1,424,596	$1,353,366	$1,840,146
$0	$55,745	$438,501	$0	$0	$1,436,473	$1,364,649	$1,844,959
$0	$0	$454,624	$0	$0	$1,504,061	$1,428,858	$1,883,482
$0	$0	$473,970	$0	$0	$1,575,238	$1,496,476	$1,970,446
$0	$0	$504,388	$0	$0	$1,697,252	$1,612,389	$2,116,777
$0	$0	$412,065	$0	$0	$1,859,947	$1,766,950	$2,179,015
$0	$0	$369,669	$0	$0	$2,001,426	$1,901,355	$2,271,024
$0	$0	$336,011	$0	$0	$2,148,362	$2,040,944	$2,376,955
$0	$0	$250,114	$0	$0	$2,233,285	$2,121,620	$2,371,734
$0	$0	$189,492	$0	$0	$2,204,248	$2,094,035	$2,283,527
$0	$0	$95,791	$0	$0	$2,209,180	$2,098,721	$2,194,511
$0	$0	$0	$1,392,992	$138,608	$2,229,491	$1,979,408	$1,979,408
$0	$0	$0	$1,495,377	$263,890	$2,282,108	$1,904,113	$1,904,113
$0	$0	$0	$1,636,690	$409,463	$2,335,483	$1,809,246	**$1,809,246**

Exhibit 5.12
*Retirement Plan with Tenure Payment Strategy for HECM
Case Study for Market Data, 1962-1995*

	Expenses and Taxes			Income Sources			Account Distributions		
Year	Pre-Tax Expenses	Income Taxes	Total Expenses	Total Income	Social Security	HECM Distribution	Taxable	Tax-Deferred	Tax Exempt
1962	$77,000	$0	$77,000	$77,000	$0	$9,920	$67,080	$0	$0
1963	$77,893	$0	$77,893	$77,893	$0	$9,920	$67,973	$0	$0
1964	$79,010	$0	$79,010	$79,010	$0	$9,920	$69,090	$0	$0
1965	$79,680	$0	$79,680	$79,680	$0	$9,920	$69,760	$0	$0
1966	$81,020	$0	$81,020	$81,020	$0	$9,920	$53,658	$17,442	$0
1967	$83,477	$1,047	$84,523	$84,523	$49,350	$9,920	$0	$25,253	$0
1968	$86,157	$1,225	$87,381	$87,381	$51,150	$9,920	$0	$26,311	$0
1969	$89,507	$1,447	$90,954	$90,954	$53,400	$9,920	$0	$27,634	$0
1970	$94,420	$1,774	$96,194	$96,193	$56,700	$9,920	$0	$29,574	$0
1971	$98,887	$2,070	$100,957	$100,957	$59,700	$9,920	$0	$31,337	$0
1972	$101,790	$2,263	$104,053	$104,053	$61,650	$9,920	$0	$32,483	$0
1973	$105,140	$2,486	$107,626	$107,626	$63,900	$9,920	$0	$33,806	$0
1974	$114,073	$3,079	$117,152	$117,152	$69,900	$9,920	$0	$37,332	$0
1975	$116,357	$1,625	$117,982	$117,982	$78,150	$9,920	$0	$29,912	$0
1976	$124,173	$2,144	$126,318	$126,318	$83,400	$9,920	$0	$32,998	$0
1977	$130,650	$2,575	$133,225	$133,225	$87,750	$9,920	$0	$35,555	$0
1978	$139,583	$3,168	$142,752	$142,751	$93,750	$9,920	$0	$39,081	$0
1979	$152,537	$4,029	$156,565	$156,565	$102,450	$9,920	$0	$44,195	$0
1980	$173,753	$5,438	$179,191	$179,191	$116,700	$9,920	$0	$52,571	$0
1981	$194,300	$7,096	$201,396	$201,396	$130,500	$9,920	$0	$60,976	$0
1982	$210,603	$8,558	$219,161	$219,161	$141,450	$9,920	$0	$67,791	$0
1983	$218,420	$9,259	$227,679	$227,679	$146,700	$9,920	$0	$71,059	$0
1984	$227,577	$10,080	$237,657	$237,657	$152,850	$9,920	$0	$74,887	$0
1985	$235,617	$10,801	$246,418	$246,418	$158,250	$9,920	$0	$78,248	$0
1986	$244,773	$11,622	$256,396	$256,396	$164,400	$9,920	$0	$82,076	$0
1987	$248,347	$11,943	$260,290	$260,289	$166,800	$9,920	$0	$83,570	$0
1988	$258,397	$12,844	$271,241	$271,241	$173,550	$9,920	$0	$87,771	$0
1989	$270,457	$13,926	$284,382	$284,382	$181,650	$9,920	$0	$92,812	$0
1990	$284,527	$15,188	$299,714	$299,714	$191,100	$9,920	$0	$98,694	$0
1991	$300,607	$16,630	$317,236	$317,236	$201,900	$9,920	$0	$105,416	$0
1992	$308,423	$17,331	$325,754	$325,754	$207,150	$9,920	$0	$108,684	$0
1993	$318,473	$18,232	$336,705	$336,705	$213,900	$9,920	$0	$112,885	$0
1994	$326,513	$18,953	$345,466	$345,466	$219,300	$9,920	$0	$116,246	$0
1995	$335,670	$19,774	$355,444	$355,444	$225,450	$9,920	$0	$120,074	$0

Exhibit 5.12 continued…

Remaining Investment Wealth			Housing Wealth				
Taxable	Tax-Deferred	Tax Exempt	Principal Limit	HECM Balance	Home Value	Net Housing Wealth	Net Legacy
$224,622	$513,893	$100,763	$159,904	$30,768	$450,000	$396,732	$1,107,537
$176,964	$580,539	$113,831	$170,298	$43,333	$451,450	$385,545	$1,111,744
$119,817	$644,817	$126,435	$182,372	$57,028	$460,634	$380,574	$1,110,438
$53,658	$691,199	$135,529	$195,977	$71,943	$469,334	$373,925	$1,081,511
$0	$660,654	$132,893	$212,517	$88,772	$475,618	$363,065	$991,449
$0	$689,793	$144,270	$230,688	$107,130	$479,968	$348,840	$1,010,454
$0	$709,924	$154,368	$251,842	$127,783	$490,602	$338,288	$1,025,099
$0	$632,055	$143,002	$279,670	$152,919	$513,802	$335,193	$952,237
$0	$673,862	$159,945	$311,525	$181,387	$552,470	$343,460	$1,008,802
$0	$717,290	$178,556	$338,503	$207,874	$593,555	$356,004	$1,072,528
$0	$763,379	$199,043	$364,297	$234,390	$619,173	$353,825	$1,125,402
$0	$667,130	$182,007	$404,114	$271,013	$634,157	$331,436	$1,013,791
$0	$559,812	$161,782	$450,143	$312,931	$662,675	$316,610	$898,251
$0	$664,970	$203,020	$496,238	$355,911	$737,395	$344,615	$1,046,362
$0	$702,928	$225,814	$539,410	$397,658	$776,208	$339,740	$1,092,750
$0	$637,781	$215,801	$584,073	$441,325	$842,833	$359,366	$1,053,503
$0	$657,541	$237,011	$647,037	$499,890	$967,853	$419,571	$1,149,737
$0	$672,046	$259,693	$720,734	$567,877	$1,123,602	$499,545	$1,263,273
$0	$716,033	$300,172	$802,826	$643,608	$1,267,766	$560,770	$1,397,967
$0	$633,573	$290,327	$894,267	$727,965	$1,358,905	$562,995	$1,328,502
$0	$752,911	$386,352	$996,125	$821,930	$1,424,596	$531,436	$1,482,471
$0	$773,888	$438,501	$1,109,583	$926,597	$1,436,473	$438,052	$1,456,969
$0	$767,870	$481,704	$1,235,965	$1,043,187	$1,504,061	$385,671	$1,443,277
$0	$866,411	$605,192	$1,376,247	$1,172,634	$1,575,238	$323,842	$1,578,842
$0	$1,005,114	$775,544	$1,518,138	$1,304,476	$1,697,252	$307,914	$1,837,294
$0	$898,059	$755,779	$1,658,565	$1,435,977	$1,859,947	$330,972	$1,760,296
$0	$915,408	$853,828	$1,834,871	$1,599,596	$2,001,426	$301,759	$1,842,142
$0	$984,115	$1,021,480	$2,043,863	$1,792,840	$2,148,362	$248,104	$2,007,670
$0	$912,904	$1,053,186	$2,276,659	$2,008,094	$2,233,285	$113,526	$1,851,391
$0	$1,010,603	$1,318,104	$2,502,503	$2,218,201	$2,204,248	$0	$2,076,056
$0	$979,336	$1,431,244	$2,675,426	$2,382,084	$2,209,180	$0	$2,165,746
$0	$971,310	$1,604,457	$2,847,724	$2,546,049	$2,229,491	$0	$2,332,940
$0	$833,233	$1,563,492	$3,057,031	$2,743,833	$2,282,108	$0	$2,188,417
$0	$930,367	$2,039,688	$3,345,921	$3,013,983	$2,335,483	$0	**$2,737,463**

Exhibit 5.13
Retirement Plan with Coordinated Portfolio Strategy for HECM
Case Study for Market Data, 1962-1995

Year	Expenses and Taxes			Income Sources			Account Distributions		
	Pre-Tax Expenses	Income Taxes	Total Expenses	Total Income	Social Security	HECM Distribution	Taxable	Tax-Deferred	Tax Exempt
1962	$77,000	$0	$77,000	$77,000	$0	$0	$77,000	$0	$0
1963	$77,893	$0	$77,893	$77,893	$0	$38,947	$38,947	$0	$0
1964	$79,010	$0	$79,010	$79,010	$0	$39,505	$39,505	$0	$0
1965	$79,680	$0	$79,680	$79,680	$0	$0	$79,680	$0	$0
1966	$81,020	$0	$81,020	$81,020	$0	$0	$81,020	$0	$0
1967	$83,477	$0	$83,477	$83,477	$49,350	$17,063	$17,063	$0	$0
1968	$86,157	$0	$86,157	$86,157	$51,150	$17,503	$5,774	$11,729	$0
1969	$89,507	$4,452	$93,959	$93,959	$53,400	$0	$0	$40,559	$0
1970	$94,420	$0	$94,420	$94,420	$56,700	$18,860	$0	$18,860	$0
1971	$98,887	$0	$98,887	$98,887	$59,700	$19,593	$0	$19,593	$0
1972	$101,790	$5,554	$107,344	$107,343	$61,650	$0	$0	$45,693	$0
1973	$105,140	$5,854	$110,994	$110,994	$63,900	$0	$0	$47,094	$0
1974	$114,073	$6,655	$120,729	$120,728	$69,900	$0	$0	$50,828	$0
1975	$116,357	$2,325	$118,681	$118,681	$78,150	$6,839	$0	$33,692	$0
1976	$124,173	$4,617	$128,790	$128,790	$83,400	$0	$0	$45,390	$0
1977	$130,650	$5,198	$135,848	$135,848	$87,750	$0	$0	$48,098	$0
1978	$139,583	$3,653	$143,236	$143,236	$93,750	$7,786	$0	$41,700	$0
1979	$152,537	$7,161	$159,697	$159,697	$102,450	$0	$0	$57,247	$0
1980	$173,753	$9,063	$182,817	$182,816	$116,700	$0	$0	$66,116	$0
1981	$194,300	$10,906	$205,206	$205,206	$130,500	$0	$0	$74,706	$0
1982	$210,603	$12,368	$222,971	$222,971	$141,450	$0	$0	$81,521	$0
1983	$218,420	$13,069	$231,489	$231,489	$146,700	$0	$0	$84,789	$0
1984	$227,577	$13,890	$241,467	$241,467	$152,850	$0	$0	$88,617	$0
1985	$235,617	$14,611	$250,228	$250,228	$158,250	$0	$0	$91,978	$0
1986	$244,773	$15,433	$260,206	$260,206	$164,400	$0	$0	$95,806	$0
1987	$248,347	$15,753	$264,100	$264,100	$166,800	$0	$0	$97,300	$0
1988	$258,397	$16,654	$275,051	$275,051	$173,550	$0	$0	$101,501	$0
1989	$270,457	$17,736	$288,193	$288,192	$181,650	$0	$0	$106,542	$0
1990	$284,527	$18,998	$303,524	$303,524	$191,100	$0	$0	$112,424	$0
1991	$300,607	$20,440	$321,046	$321,046	$201,900	$0	$0	$119,146	$0
1992	$308,423	$21,141	$329,564	$329,564	$207,150	$0	$0	$122,414	$0
1993	$318,473	$22,042	$340,515	$340,515	$213,900	$0	$0	$126,615	$0
1994	$326,513	$22,763	$349,276	$349,276	$219,300	$0	$0	$129,976	$0
1995	$335,670	$23,584	$359,254	$359,254	$225,450	$0	$0	$133,804	$0

Exhibit 5.13 continued…

Remaining Investment Wealth			Housing Wealth				
Taxable	Tax-Deferred	Tax Exempt	Principal Limit	HECM Balance	Home Value	Net Housing Wealth	Net Legacy
$214,626	$513,893	$100,763	$159,904	$20,214	$450,000	$407,286	$1,108,095
$198,463	$580,539	$113,831	$170,298	$63,006	$451,450	$365,871	$1,113,570
$176,558	$644,817	$126,435	$182,372	$109,779	$460,634	$327,823	$1,114,428
$103,846	$691,199	$135,529	$195,977	$117,969	$469,334	$327,899	$1,085,673
$22,382	$677,756	$132,893	$212,517	$127,925	$475,618	$323,911	$987,504
$5,774	$735,775	$144,270	$230,688	$157,385	$479,968	$298,584	$1,000,459
$0	$774,726	$154,368	$251,842	$190,926	$490,602	$275,146	$1,010,558
$0	$680,114	$143,002	$279,670	$212,023	$513,802	$276,089	$929,177
$0	$739,597	$159,945	$311,525	$257,181	$552,470	$267,666	$982,309
$0	$803,784	$178,556	$338,503	$300,743	$593,555	$263,135	$1,044,529
$0	$845,072	$199,043	$364,297	$323,659	$619,173	$264,555	$1,097,402
$0	$729,679	$182,007	$404,114	$359,035	$634,157	$243,414	$972,680
$0	$603,414	$161,782	$450,143	$399,929	$662,675	$229,611	$843,954
$0	$714,943	$203,020	$496,238	$448,421	$737,395	$252,104	$991,331
$0	$744,728	$225,814	$539,410	$487,434	$776,208	$249,964	$1,034,324
$0	$665,740	$215,801	$584,073	$527,793	$842,833	$272,898	$988,004
$0	$685,373	$237,011	$647,037	$593,315	$967,853	$326,145	$1,077,185
$0	$688,240	$259,693	$720,734	$660,894	$1,123,602	$406,529	$1,182,402
$0	$719,095	$300,172	$802,826	$736,170	$1,267,766	$468,208	$1,307,702
$0	$623,255	$290,327	$894,267	$820,019	$1,358,905	$470,940	$1,228,709
$0	$720,909	$386,352	$996,125	$913,419	$1,424,596	$439,946	$1,366,980
$0	$721,983	$438,501	$1,109,583	$1,017,458	$1,436,473	$347,192	$1,327,180
$0	$695,768	$481,704	$1,235,965	$1,133,346	$1,504,061	$295,511	$1,299,041
$0	$758,575	$605,192	$1,376,247	$1,261,981	$1,575,238	$234,495	$1,408,618
$0	$849,329	$775,544	$1,518,138	$1,392,091	$1,697,252	$220,298	$1,632,840
$0	$732,864	$755,779	$1,658,565	$1,520,860	$1,859,947	$246,090	$1,551,517
$0	$713,271	$853,828	$1,834,871	$1,682,527	$2,001,426	$218,827	$1,607,608
$0	$725,862	$1,021,480	$2,043,863	$1,874,167	$2,148,362	$166,777	$1,732,653
$0	$632,479	$1,053,186	$2,276,659	$2,087,635	$2,233,285	$33,986	$1,561,531
$0	$642,456	$1,318,104	$2,502,503	$2,294,728	$2,204,248	$0	$1,799,946
$0	$564,680	$1,431,244	$2,675,426	$2,453,294	$2,209,180	$0	$1,854,754
$0	$491,080	$1,604,457	$2,847,724	$2,611,286	$2,229,491	$0	$1,972,767
$0	$351,884	$1,563,492	$3,057,031	$2,803,215	$2,282,108	$0	$1,827,406
$0	$284,501	$2,039,688	$3,345,921	$3,068,119	$2,335,483	$0	**$2,253,064**

Exhibit 5.14
Coordinated Portfolio Strategy with Voluntary Repayments for HECM
Case Study for Market Data, 1962-1995

	Expenses and Taxes			Income Sources			Account Distributions		
Year	Pre-Tax Expenses	Income Taxes	Total Expenses	Total Income	Social Security	HECM Distribution	Taxable	Tax-Deferred	Tax Exempt
1962	$77,000	$0	$77,000	$77,000	$0	$0	$77,000	$0	$0
1963	$77,893	$0	$77,893	$77,893	$0	$38,947	$38,947	$0	$0
1964	$79,010	$0	$79,010	$79,010	$0	$39,505	$39,505	$0	$0
1965	$79,680	$0	$79,680	$79,680	$0	$0	$79,680	$0	$0
1966	$81,020	$0	$81,020	$81,020	$0	$0	$81,020	$0	$0
1967	$83,477	$0	$83,477	$83,477	$49,350	$17,063	$17,063	$0	$0
1968	$86,157	$0	$86,157	$86,157	$51,150	$17,503	$5,774	$11,729	$0
1969	$89,507	$4,452	$93,959	$93,959	$53,400	$0	$0	$40,559	$0
1970	$94,420	$0	$94,420	$94,420	$56,700	$18,860	$0	$18,860	$0
1971	$98,887	$0	$98,887	$98,887	$59,700	$19,593	$0	$19,593	$0
1972	$101,790	$5,554	$107,344	$107,343	$61,650	$0	$0	$45,693	$0
1973	$105,140	$5,854	$110,994	$110,994	$63,900	$0	$0	$47,094	$0
1974	$114,073	$6,655	$120,729	$120,728	$69,900	$0	$0	$50,828	$0
1975	$116,357	$2,325	$118,681	$118,681	$78,150	$6,839	$0	$33,692	$0
1976	$124,173	$4,617	$128,790	$128,790	$83,400	$0	$0	$45,390	$0
1977	$130,650	$5,198	$135,848	$135,848	$87,750	$0	$0	$48,098	$0
1978	$139,583	$3,653	$143,236	$143,236	$93,750	$7,786	$0	$41,700	$0
1979	$152,537	$7,161	$159,697	$159,697	$102,450	$0	$0	$57,247	$0
1980	$173,753	$9,063	$182,817	$182,816	$116,700	$0	$0	$66,116	$0
1981	$194,300	$10,906	$205,206	$205,206	$130,500	$0	$0	$74,706	$0
1982	$210,603	$12,368	$222,971	$222,971	$141,450	$0	$0	$81,521	$0
1983	$218,420	$13,069	$231,489	$231,489	$146,700	$0	$0	$84,789	$0
1984	$227,577	$23,865	$251,441	$251,441	$152,850	-$35,484	$0	$134,075	$0
1985	$235,617	$15,585	$251,202	$251,202	$158,250	-$2,535	$0	$95,486	$0
1986	$244,773	$52,969	$297,742	$297,742	$164,400	-$171,620	$0	$304,962	$0
1987	$248,347	$44,938	$293,285	$293,284	$166,800	-$145,795	$0	$272,280	$0
1988	$258,397	$16,654	$275,051	$275,051	$173,550	$0	$0	$101,501	$0
1989	$270,457	$17,736	$288,193	$288,192	$181,650	$0	$0	$106,542	$0
1990	$284,527	$352	$284,878	$284,878	$191,100	$0	$0	$29,032	$64,747
1991	$300,607	$0	$300,607	$300,607	$201,900	$0	$0	$0	$98,707
1992	$308,423	$0	$308,423	$308,423	$207,150	$0	$0	$0	$101,273
1993	$318,473	$0	$318,473	$318,473	$213,900	$0	$0	$0	$104,573
1994	$326,513	$0	$326,513	$326,513	$219,300	$0	$0	$0	$107,213
1995	$335,670	$0	$335,670	$335,670	$225,450	$0	$0	$0	$110,220

Exhibit 5.14 continued…

Remaining Investment Wealth			Housing Wealth				Net Legacy
Taxable	Tax-Deferred	Tax Exempt	Principal Limit	HECM Balance	Home Value	Net Housing Wealth	
$214,626	$513,893	$100,763	$159,904	$20,214	$450,000	$407,286	$1,108,095
$198,463	$580,539	$113,831	$170,298	$63,006	$451,450	$365,871	$1,113,570
$176,558	$644,817	$126,435	$182,372	$109,779	$460,634	$327,823	$1,114,428
$103,846	$691,199	$135,529	$195,977	$117,969	$469,334	$327,899	$1,085,673
$22,382	$677,756	$132,893	$212,517	$127,925	$475,618	$323,911	$987,504
$5,774	$735,775	$144,270	$230,688	$157,385	$479,968	$298,584	$1,000,459
$0	$774,726	$154,368	$251,842	$190,926	$490,602	$275,146	$1,010,558
$0	$680,114	$143,002	$279,670	$212,023	$513,802	$276,089	$929,177
$0	$739,597	$159,945	$311,525	$257,181	$552,470	$267,666	$982,309
$0	$803,784	$178,556	$338,503	$300,743	$593,555	$263,135	$1,044,529
$0	$845,072	$199,043	$364,297	$323,659	$619,173	$264,555	$1,097,402
$0	$729,679	$182,007	$404,114	$359,035	$634,157	$243,414	$972,680
$0	$603,414	$161,782	$450,143	$399,929	$662,675	$229,611	$843,954
$0	$714,943	$203,020	$496,238	$448,421	$737,395	$252,104	$991,331
$0	$744,728	$225,814	$539,410	$487,434	$776,208	$249,964	$1,034,324
$0	$665,740	$215,801	$584,073	$527,793	$842,833	$272,898	$988,004
$0	$685,373	$237,011	$647,037	$593,315	$967,853	$326,145	$1,077,185
$0	$688,240	$259,693	$720,734	$660,894	$1,123,602	$406,529	$1,182,402
$0	$719,095	$300,172	$802,826	$736,170	$1,267,766	$468,208	$1,307,702
$0	$623,255	$290,327	$894,267	$820,019	$1,358,905	$470,940	$1,228,709
$0	$720,909	$386,352	$996,125	$913,419	$1,424,596	$439,946	$1,366,980
$0	$721,983	$438,501	$1,109,583	$1,017,458	$1,436,473	$347,192	$1,327,180
$0	$645,831	$481,704	$1,235,965	$1,093,821	$1,504,061	$335,037	$1,301,114
$0	$691,429	$605,192	$1,376,247	$1,215,147	$1,575,238	$281,329	$1,405,092
$0	$495,251	$775,544	$1,518,138	$1,151,114	$1,697,252	$461,275	$1,608,258
$0	$217,289	$755,779	$1,658,565	$1,098,311	$1,859,947	$668,639	$1,587,385
$0	$130,809	$853,828	$1,834,871	$1,215,061	$2,001,426	$686,294	$1,638,228
$0	$29,032	$1,021,480	$2,043,863	$1,353,457	$2,148,362	$687,487	$1,730,741
$0	$0	$986,430	$2,276,659	$1,507,615	$2,233,285	$614,005	$1,600,435
$0	$0	$1,111,020	$2,502,503	$1,657,171	$2,204,248	$436,864	$1,547,885
$0	$0	$1,096,419	$2,675,426	$1,771,681	$2,209,180	$327,039	$1,423,458
$0	$0	$1,111,881	$2,847,724	$1,885,778	$2,229,491	$232,239	$1,344,120
$0	$0	$979,017	$3,057,031	$2,024,382	$2,282,108	$143,620	$1,122,637
$0	$0	$1,133,408	$3,345,921	$2,215,686	$2,335,483	$3,023	**$1,136,431**

Chapter 6: Debt Coordination for Housing

Coordinating housing-related spending with the investment portfolio and a reverse mortgage can be a critical step in a structurally sound retirement plan. Fairway Independent Mortgage Corporation provided me with data about how their client base used HECMs in 2021. Fairway found that 72 percent of the reverse mortgages they initiated through financial planners were primarily intended to refinance existing mortgages carried into retirement. As for the remainder, 21 percent opened a reverse mortgage to set up a growing line of credit, 4 percent used the tenure payment option for the HECM, and 3 percent used the HECM for Purchase.

Though most of the research on HECMs is about portfolio coordination strategies, this chapter covers the most popular real-world use for the HECM program: refinancing a traditional mortgage to eliminate the burden of making fixed mortgage payments in early retirement, when one is most exposed to sequence-of-return risk. The important question is whether the ability to mitigate sequence-of-return risk by refinancing the mortgage with a HECM and removing the fixed mortgage expenditure from the budget in the pivotal early retirement years is beneficial enough to offset the HECM's costs.

This issue of needing to make fixed payments on debt, which raises cash flow needs in retirement, goes beyond just mortgage payments. We can learn about this with data crunched by the Urban Institute from the 2019 Survey of Consumer Finances. They found that for households with the head aged 65 to 74, 72.4 percent were still carrying debt. This was up from 51.5 percent in 1989. Meanwhile, for those age 75 and older, 55 percent carried debt, compared to 21.2 percent in 1989.

We also consider using the HECM for Purchase to purchase a new home in retirement. We will compare funding part of a new home's cost with a HECM for Purchase against alternatives, such as paying cash for the home or obtaining a traditional 15-year mortgage.

For those not carrying a substantial mortgage into retirement, an additional simple HECM use related to housing is to fund home renovations, which better support the ability to age in place. Possible upgrades, as listed in Chapter 2, can help retirees remain in their homes for longer, reducing pressure to move to an institutionalized long-term-care setting. Our focus in this chapter, though, is on situations in which a retiree is contemplating whether it's better to use a HECM or carry a traditional mortgage into retirement.

Carrying a Mortgage into Retirement

More Americans are entering retirement while still carrying a traditional mortgage. The Urban Institute found that for 65 to 74 year olds, the percentage who held a traditional mortgage rose from less than 30 percent in 1989 to more than 40 percent in 2019. For those age 75 and older, households with mortgages increased from under 10 percent in 1989 to more than 25 percent in 2019. Median mortgage balances were just under $100,000.

For those approaching or already in retirement with a mortgage, it is worth considering whether to take action to extinguish these payments. This decision involves the general points made about pre-paying a mortgage earlier in life, but the decision may come out differently as the nature of investment risk and volatility grows when one enters retirement. After reaching age 62, the HECM also presents an option to refinance the mortgage and remove those fixed mortgage payments from the retirement budget.

The general arguments in support of maintaining a mortgage, even when assets are available to extinguish it, relate to the ability to leverage the investment portfolio for greater growth and benefit from the tax deduction on mortgage interest for acquisition debt.

When we think about risk tolerance and asset allocation in a broader perspective, beyond an investment portfolio, a mortgage is effectively a "negative bond." It represents a bond you have issued instead of a bond you own. Instead of receiving interest like a typical bond, interest is charged to the borrower on the outstanding mortgage balance at the rate set by the mortgage. Paying down mortgage principal can be framed as investing in an asset yielding a rate of return equal to the mortgage rate.

Consider a very basic example of a fixed rate mortgage with a 3.5 percent interest rate. After making an obligated mortgage payment, suppose you have an extra $1,000 of available cash. For this example, there is already an established emergency fund and no other debt, such as credit cards or student loans, with higher interest rates. If you use the $1,000 to make a voluntary principal payment on the mortgage, it reduces the interest growth on $1,000 of principal on an annual basis by 3.5 percent. We can compare that to other investment alternatives. If you were to invest that $1,000 in a CD paying 1 percent, then you would be better off paying down the mortgage instead. If there were another safe investment paying 6 percent, then you would be better off investing in the asset earning 6 percent instead of voluntarily paying down the mortgage balance that "earns" 3.5 percent.

An important consideration, though, is that the potential to earn a higher return than the mortgage interest rate will generally require accepting risk. There will rarely be a safe investment earning more than mortgage interest rates, except perhaps if someone locked in a mortgage at a low rate and then interest rates later rise.

When risk is involved, the decision to pre-pay a mortgage requires a consideration of risk tolerance. Holding a mortgage means holding a negative bond and leveraging the home equity to seek the potential for a higher investment return. The asset allocation is effectively more aggressive with a mortgage. Risk tolerance guides this pre-pay decision, with the understanding that risk tolerance can decline at retirement, and investment volatility can have a bigger impact at retirement because of the amplified sequence-of-return risk that distributions create. What's more, once work stops, paying a mortgage requires taking distributions from assets. If this involves distributions from a tax-deferred account, then adjusted gross income may be increased in ways that cause other undesired tax consequences, such as triggering taxes on Social Security benefits.

Another matter relates to the potential tax advantages of holding a mortgage. Interest on acquisition debt, which is debt to build, acquire, or substantially improve a home, can be deducted. But to be deductible, itemized deductions need to exceed the standard deduction. After the changes to the tax code made in late 2017, it has become increasingly difficult to itemize. When the standard deduction is taken, there is no tax benefit provided from mortgage interest deductibility. Even when one itemizes, only the amount that exceeds the standard deduction receives any real tax benefit. This may be less likely, too, as the portion of mortgage payments allocated to interest declines with mortgages as the principal is re-paid over time. By the time retirement arrives, most of the mortgage payment may be to pay down principal instead of interest, further making a deduction less likely. In retirement, paying a mortgage can mostly mean shifting assets from the investment portfolio to home equity.

Mortgage debt in retirement presents an additional planning challenge. For retirement distributions, fixed payments related to paying off debt create a strain for retirees, due to the fact that heightened withdrawal needs trigger greater exposure to sequence-of-return risk. Exposure rises because the debt payments are fixed and require greater distributions than otherwise; if there is a market decline early in retirement, the portfolio is further strained as an even greater percentage of what is left in the portfolio must be taken to meet these fixed expenses.

With the attendant diversification impacts, sequence-of-return risk amplification, and potential tax headaches, is there a better option than simply carrying a traditional mortgage into retirement?

The general idea is that a reverse mortgage used primarily to refinance an existing mortgage creates more flexibility for distribution needs from the investment portfolio, by removing a fixed expense from household budgeting in the key early-retirement years. During preretirement, it is common to pay off the mortgage more slowly in hopes that investment returns will outpace the borrowing costs on the mortgage. This approach becomes riskier in retirement, as distribution needs heighten the retiree's vulnerability and exposure to market volatility. In addition, a changing tax situation with the loss of wages and the dwindling mortgage balance in retirement could mean losing potential tax deductions for mortgage interest.

The benefit of replacing a mortgage with a reverse mortgage, then, is the reduced exposure to sequence risk. However, it is also important to note that the growth rate on the reverse mortgage loan balance can exceed the interest rate on the preexisting mortgage, especially if interest rates rise from their current levels. One must weigh the increased flexibility and reduced expenditures in early retirement against the possibility that the final legacy value for assets could be hurt if the HECM loan balance is not repaid for many years. Whether the legacy increases or decreases when using a reverse mortgage in this way also depends on the performance of the investment portfolio, which can benefit from greater potential growth due to lower distribution needs placed on it.

We can analyze these complexities with the same case study from the previous chapter, but with modifications to have a traditional mortgage still in place at the time of retirement. For a retiree carrying a traditional mortgage into retirement, the question becomes what to do with it. I consider two options for those reaching retirement with a traditional mortgage still in place:

1. Carry the mortgage into retirement, making the required ongoing payments until the mortgage has been fully paid off. Open a HECM as a last resort—only if portfolio assets are depleted later in retirement.

2. Use a HECM to refinance the mortgage balance. If any principal limit remains after covering the mortgage debt, use this remainder to fund a tenure payment for the couple. In cases where the initial principal limit is less than the remaining mortgage balance and upfront costs, cover the remainder with a distribution from the investment portfolio. It is called "short to close" when additional cash will be needed to extinguish the mortgage balance beyond the principal limit capacity to allow the HECM to be opened. Upfront costs are assumed to be the full $19,000 described before. But with these high utilization cases that involve significant initial draws from the HECM, it may be possible to negotiate lower upfront costs from the lender.

These possibilities can provide a sense of how keeping a mortgage compares with using a HECM to refinance it. By refinancing the existing mortgage with a HECM, one could voluntarily continue making the same monthly payments on the loan balance of the reverse mortgage to reduce it and increase the credit line for future use. Unlike with a traditional mortgage, these voluntary repayments can be stopped without triggering foreclosure. Voluntary payments can be made strategically when markets are performing well and then stopped when it is necessary to sell assets at a loss to make payments. I do not further consider this possibility.

Our case study here is based on the previous chapter, with a few adjustments to account for the fact that a mortgage balance remains at the start of retirement. For this case study, we assume that the home is currently worth $450,000. It was purchased 20 years prior. Its price at that time is discounted by the Case-Shiller home price index to reflect housing price changes during those 20 years. With that purchase price, a traditional fixed-rate 30-year mortgage with a 20 percent down payment was taken using a mortgage rate equal to 2 percent plus the 10-year Treasury rate at that time.

At the present, the couple has 10 years left on their mortgage. Their annual mortgage payments and the mortgage balance remaining at retirement will vary for each of the simulations as it depends on the interest rate and housing price dynamics over different 20-year periods. For situations where data is needed before 1890 to understand what happened prior to the starting point for retirement, I assumed housing price growth of 3.7 percent applied in any prior years, and I did use actual 10-Year Treasury rate data, which is available since 1871. For one case (1890 retirement), the 10-year Treasury rate in 1870 is needed, and for this I assumed that the 1871 interest rate also applied in that year.

Exhibit 6.1
Comparing the HECM Refinance to Keeping the Mortgage & Last-Resort Strategy
Net Real Legacy Wealth (HECM Refinance – Keep & Last Resort)

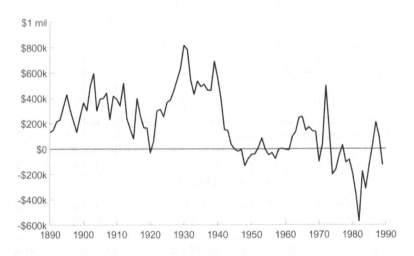

I make one final adjustment to help offset the additional liability created through the remaining mortgage balance relative to the previous chapter. As noted, the remaining mortgage balance at retirement will be different in each of the simulations, but its average value across all 100 simulations is $118,339. To help offset the liability so that retirement success rates do not fall by too much, I increased the value of the taxable account and its cost balance by this amount. Initial investment assets are now $1,018,339, instead of $900,000. Otherwise, case study assumptions are the same.

Exhibit 6.1 provides the results for this comparison, showing the difference in net real legacy wealth from the historical simulations for refinancing the traditional mortgage with a HECM (which comes out ahead when legacy wealth is above $0), against the strategy of maintaining the mortgage into retirement and only treating the HECM as a last-resort option (which comes out ahead when legacy wealth is negative). The HECM refinancing strategy supports a greater net legacy in 72 percent of the historical simulations, with an average real gain to legacy of $187,422. As is common, 1982 provides the case when the refinancing strategy worked least well. In this case, the HECM could finance so little and the large cash payment required took funds out of the market that could have benefited from the significant market growth in those early retirement years. Otherwise, this exhibit provides compelling evidence for using the HECM to improve retirements.

Exhibit 6.2
Comparing the HECM Refinance to Keeping the Mortgage & Last-Resort Strategy
Net Real Legacy Wealth

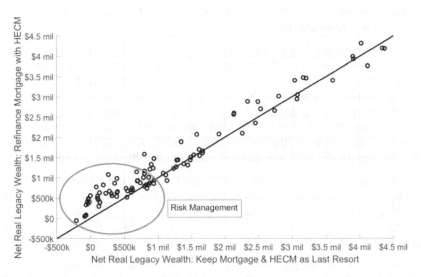

Generally, keeping the traditional mortgage creates sequence risk, since portfolio distributions are higher in early retirement to cover mortgage payments as well. This locks in greater losses for the retirement plan after a market decline. We can further confirm this with Exhibit 6.2, which compares net legacy wealth in absolute terms for the two strategies. The exhibit shows consistent outperformance for the HECM refinancing strategy in the lower-left portion of the exhibit, which highlights how the HECM refinancing strategy helps to better manage retirement risk. The HECM helps preserve assets at the times that it matters most, which is when the retirement is in greater jeopardy. Its underperformance tends to happen in the stronger market environments that lead to larger absolute wealth for both strategies. The HECM refinancing provides a stronger opportunity to preserve legacy assets after meeting spending goals, while also reducing retirement risk.

HECM for Purchase

The HECM for Purchase program began in 2009 as a way to use a reverse mortgage to purchase a new home. The federal government saw enough people using a costlier and more complicated two-step process—obtaining a traditional mortgage to purchase the home and then using a reverse mortgage to refinance the first one—that it sought to simplify the process and reduce the costs. The HECM for Purchase program allows fewer distributions from the investment portfolio to pay for the home because a greater portion of the home's cost can be financed by the HECM.

The HECM for Purchase program can be used to either downsize or upsize a retirement home. For those downsizing, the HECM for Purchase could free up more assets from the sale of the previous home to be used for other purposes. For those upsizing with the financial resources to manage this sustainably and *responsibly*, the HECM for Purchase could allow for a more expensive home—especially considering the possibility that qualifying for a traditional mortgage can be more difficult after retiring.

Should the borrower live in the home long enough, the loan balance may grow to exceed the value of the home, setting its non-recourse aspect into motion. In this situation, one could interpret the HECM for Purchase program as providing housing services for as long as the borrower remains eligible, for a total cost equal to the portion of the home value and upfront costs not covered by the HECM. Should the borrower leave the home while the loan balance is still less than the home value, the home could be sold with any remaining equity still available to the borrower after the loan is repaid.

In terms of coordinating the use of debt for housing, not having to make a monthly mortgage payment reduces the household's fixed costs and provides potential relief for the need to spend down investments. The HECM for Purchase option can be analyzed relative to paying outright for the home with other assets or opening a 15-year mortgage, if still feasible.

To consider the HECM for Purchase case, I add a slight modification to the scenario described in Chapter 5. Rather than already owning a $450,000 home, the couple is now at the point of purchasing this home. To keep asset levels the same, the value of their taxable account and its cost basis both increase by $450,000. The couple considers three options:

1. Pay cash for the home. Open the HECM only as a last resort. This makes the strategy equivalent to the last-resort strategy from the previous chapter.

2. Open a 15-year fixed-rate traditional mortgage with 20 percent down. The fixed rate on the mortgage is the 10-year Treasury rate plus 1 percent. Open the HECM only as a last resort.

3. Use the HECM for Purchase to cover as much of the home cost as allowed and pay cash for the remainder. The HECM has the same parameters as before: $19,000 of upfront costs and a 2.5 percent margin rate. There is no additional line of credit available with this strategy, since the entirety goes toward funding the home purchase.

Because the story is generally the same, I can describe the results for these strategies without providing additional exhibits. Using the HECM for Purchase strategy to fund a portion of the home's purchase price provides a larger net legacy than paying cash for the home, in 75 percent of the historical cases. On average, the HECM for Purchase increases the net real legacy value of assets by $121,301. In addition, the HECM for Purchase strategy provides a larger net legacy than taking out a 15-year traditional mortgage, in 69 percent of the historical cases. Though this percentage is slightly less, the average net real legacy value is $161,340 more when using the HECM for Purchase strategy. Using the traditional mortgage creates more volatility for outcomes compared to paying cash. It works less well when markets are down in the early retirement years, since losses are incurred before mortgage payments are made, but it works better when markets perform well in the early retirement years.

In general, the HECM for Purchase strategy provides a viable option for those thinking about moving more permanently into an eligible home during their retirement. By funding a portion of the home purchase through the HECM, the investment portfolio maintains more assets at the start of retirement. This lowers the withdrawal rate from the investment portfolio needed to cover spending, setting it on a course for greater long-term sustainability and growth. Even after accounting for the costs of the reverse mortgage, retirees are mostly left in a better position by using home equity in this coordinated manner.

Chapter 7: Funding Efficiency Improvements

A reverse mortgage can help support certain long-term strategies that require accepting short-term costs to obtain long-term gains, such as:

- creating a bridge for supporting a delay in Social Security claims;
- paying the taxes on Roth conversions, or otherwise having a spending resource that will not increase adjusted gross income;
- using tenure payments as an alternative to an income annuity;
- using the HECM as an alternative source of longevity insurance; or
- maintaining an existing long-term-care insurance policy, by paying premiums from the line of credit.

For those with sufficient assets who could afford to fund these retirement efficiencies with their investment portfolios, the matter becomes determining the direction that can provide the most attractive distribution of overall outcomes for the retirement plan. Applying these sorts of strategies would become a subset of general uses for a HECM to support retirement spending in the most efficient manner. This chapter provides a detailed focus on using a reverse mortgage to support Social Security delay, to improve retirement tax efficiency, or as a replacement for an income annuity.

Building a Social Security Delay Bridge with a HECM

For the typical household in retirement, Social Security, home equity, and an investment portfolio comprise most of the available assets. When to claim Social Security benefits is a hugely important decision. As a government-backed, inflation-adjusted monthly income for life, Social Security benefits help you manage longevity risk, inflation risk, and market risk. In addition to retirement worker benefits, Social Security provides spousal, survivor, and dependent benefits from the retired worker's earnings record. The benefits also receive preferential tax treatment.

Individuals may claim their Social Security retirement benefits at any age between 62 and 70. The Full Retirement Age is now increasing above 66 and will be 67 for those born in 1960 and later. Those claiming before their full retirement age will receive a reduced benefit. Claiming after will provide delay credits and larger benefits until age 70. The decision of when to start

Social Security should be made independently from when one decides to quit working. Claiming decisions should not be taken lightly.

In my *Retirement Planning Guidebook*, I walk readers through the steps required to have a firm understanding about Social Security claiming. I discuss how Social Security benefits are calculated, and how to factor in issues such as spousal and survivor benefits for couples, dependent benefits, and benefits for divorcees. I also consider the philosophies related to claiming Social Security, including an analysis of when delaying benefits will pay off, and the validity of arguments made in favor of claiming Social Security early. I provide a detailed explanation of how to think about Social Security claiming, and I make a case that at least for the high-earning spouse in a couple, it can make a lot of sense to delay Social Security to age 70.

In this book, we jump to the punchline by looking at the impact on the retirement plan of switching the Social Security claiming age to 62 or to 70 (it was 67 in Chapter 5), and by using a term-payment from the HECM as a "Social Security delay bridge" to help relieve pressure on the investment portfolio when delaying benefits.

Before getting to that, I should mention a poorly prepared report issued by the Consumer Financial Protection Bureau (CFPB) in August 2017 called "Issue Brief: The Costs and Risks of Using a Reverse Mortgage to Delay Collecting Social Security." This report makes it seem like using a reverse mortgage to delay Social Security is a bad idea across the board. It gained a lot of press coverage, and it unfortunately may serve as the primary resource for people seeking to learn more about the matter.

I am not philosophically opposed to the CFPB. I have served as an intern at the Social Security Administration, and my original career goal, before finding my place in academics, was to become a US government economist. So I am more disappointed than anything else that this report was issued and heralded with a press release and other promotion by the CFPB.

There is a line in the conclusion of the report that is worth considering: "For consumers who have the option, working past age 62 is usually a less costly way to increase their monthly Social Security benefit than borrowing from a reverse mortgage." While it is hard to assess what "costly" means in the context of life quality, it is true that working longer, when feasible, may be the most effective way to strengthen finances for retirement.

But for those who have retired at 62, and for whom working longer is not a desirable or viable option, what is the best way to coordinate Social Security claiming, home equity, and the investment portfolio, to build an efficient overall retirement income plan? The report fails to answer this adequately; saying that a reverse mortgage is "too costly" is woefully incomplete.

What the report does is estimate the increase in total Social Security benefits (ignoring cost-of-living adjustments), obtained through a life expectancy of 85, by waiting until age 67 to claim Social Security benefits. Technically, this is not a delay of Social Security; it is just claiming at the article's assumed full retirement age, rather than claiming early. The additional benefits are compared to the costs of replacing those 5 years of "missing" benefits by taking distributions from a HECM line of credit. Reverse mortgage costs consist of the upfront fees, insurance premiums, servicing costs, and interest accumulated at the age-85 life expectancy, which the article shows are substantially higher than the net gain in Social Security benefits, leading the authors to conclude:

> We find that borrowing a reverse mortgage loan to get an increased Social Security benefit carries significant costs that generally exceed the additional lifetime amount gained from delaying Social Security. In addition, the amount that a consumer will need to borrow from a reverse mortgage loan to delay claiming Social Security benefits could negatively affect the consumer's ability to move or use their home equity to meet a large expense later in life.

These conclusions violate two of the retirement planning principles outlined in Chapter 1. First is to play the long game. We should not base our decisions about what happens at life expectancy, but rather what happens if we live well beyond it. Delaying Social Security is a form of insurance that helps support the increasing costs associated with living a long life. It provides inflation-adjusted lifetime benefits for a retiree and a surviving spouse, and these lifetime benefits will be 77 percent larger in inflation-adjusted terms for those who claim at 70 instead of at 62. The value of this insurance is missed when analysis is based only on life expectancy.

Second, and more important, the CFPB report's authors have violated principle 8, which involves working with the entire retirement balance sheet and matching assets to liabilities. We do not know the liabilities to be funded in the CFPB report; there is no given spending goal. The report also completely ignores the possible existence of an investment portfolio to help fund retirement. If retirees have expenses to meet, they must draw from their assets. For someone retired at 62, how will expenses be met? Should retirees claim Social Security early? Or build a bridge to delay Social Security using a reverse mortgage? Or delay Social Security, but fund the delay instead through distributions from an investment portfolio?

The CFPB report does not address this issue at all. All the report really seems to say is that it is better to work longer and not retire at 62. This allows expenses to be covered by labor income. Fair enough; this is a great way to bolster finances. But it simply does not address what people should do when they stop working. The CFPB's notion that the costs of a reverse mortgage exceed the benefits of Social Security delay is incomplete because it does not address how to fund the spending need, other than to assume that a person is still working. If retired, distributions from an investment portfolio also have a cost in terms of the lost compounding growth potential for those funds if they are spent instead of remaining in the portfolio.

Saying that using a reverse mortgage is too costly because it could hurt the ability to move or to use home equity for another expense ignores asset-liability matching for the retirement-spending goal. Meeting spending needs from the investment portfolio instead could potentially drain net worth faster than meeting spending needs from the reverse mortgage. We saw this already with the discussion of portfolio coordination strategies in Chapter 5. We must test their claim to see which strategy can best preserve net worth after retirement expenses are met, so that more liquidity is available later in retirement to fund a move or other expensive shock. Again, the CFPB report ignores both the spending goal and the investment portfolio, so it does not provide any meaningful conclusions about what a retiree should do.

Properly addressing this requires a more complete analysis than the CFPB report provides. We can analyze these complexities using the same case study developed in Chapter 5. In that initial investigation of portfolio coordination strategies, I assumed that the couple claimed benefits at full retirement age (67). With the worker's primary insurance amount of $2,500, this supported $30,000 of annual income for the worker and $15,000 of annual income as a spousal benefit ($45,000 total per year). The only tweak here is to consider different claiming ages for Social Security. We consider two options for those entering retirement at age 62 and no longer working:

1. Begin Social Security benefits at age 62. With the Social Security reduction factors for early claiming, the worker's benefit is reduced by 30 percent to $21,000 and the spousal benefit is reduced by 35 percent to $9,750 ($30,750 total per year). Draw the remaining amount needed to meet the overall retirement spending goal from the investment portfolio. Open a HECM only as a last resort to meet the spending goal if the investment portfolio depletes.

2. Delay claiming Social Security benefits until age 70; open a HECM at age 62 and set up an 8-year term payment to build a Social Security delay bridge that helps relieve some pressure on investment portfolio distributions while waiting for Social Security to begin. Do not voluntarily pay down the HECM loan balance. By delaying to 70, the worker is entitled to a 24 percent benefit increase ($37,200) and the spousal benefit remains at $15,000 ($52,200 total per year).

In our case study, the home is not worth enough relative to Social Security benefits for the HECM term payment to provide a full Social Security delay bridge. Total household benefits when claiming at 62 are $30,750, and Exhibit 7.1 shows the term payment available in each historical year as based on 10-year Treasury rates at that time, along with the other assumptions we used in the case study ($450,000 home, $19,000 upfront costs, 2.5 percent lender's margin, age 62). Term payments peak in 1941 at $27,507, when interest rates are the lowest. The term payment is the smallest in 1982 at $4,537, when interest rates were the highest. Additional assets could be carved out of the portfolio to further structure the Social Security delay bridge, but I will not take that extra step as the focus is to understand the role of a HECM in this process.

Exhibit 7.1
Annual HECM Term Payments (8 Years) for Social Security Delay Bridge

In Exhibit 7.2, we compare the strategy of delaying Social Security to 70 and using the HECM with an 8-year term payment, with the strategy of claiming Social Security at 62 and using the HECM only as a last resort. Delaying to 70 and using the HECM to partially bridge the missing Social Security benefits in the first 8 years provides larger net legacy wealth at age 95 in 71 percent of the historical cases, which is an average real legacy increase of $324,940. Exceptions include small shortfalls around 1920, in the mid-1940s, and a period from the mid-1970s to mid-1980s. With the case study facts, claiming at 62 and using the HECM as a last resort allows the lifetime spending goals to be met in 73 percent of the historical cases. The delay strategy with the HECM delay bridge provides a 99 percent success rate. In Chapter 5, we observed that claiming at full retirement age (67) supported a 95 percent success rate.

Delaying Social Security is a risk management technique that better protects the ability to meet retirement spending goals. We observe this with the increased success rate it provides. With managing risk, it is reasonable to expect that delaying Social Security may give up some of the upside potential if financial markets perform extremely well in retirement. That is the argument sometimes made for people to claim Social Security early and then invest their benefits in the stock market. This *can* lead to a better outcome, but it is not common and should not be expected.

Exhibit 7.2

Comparing the Claim Social Security at 70 & HECM Delay Bridge
to the Claim Social Security at 62 and Use HECM as a Last Resort
Net Real Legacy (SocSec@70 & Bridge – SocSec@62 & Last Resort)

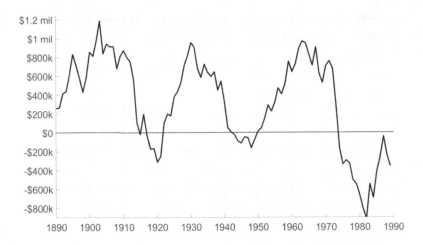

Exhibit 7.3 further confirms that delaying Social Security and using the HECM delay bridge works to manage retirement risks. This exhibit plots the net legacy wealth for the early-claiming strategy on the horizontal axis, and the net legacy wealth for the delay strategy with the HECM delay bridge on the vertical axis. This highlights that the delay strategy resulted in a negative legacy only once, and even then, the shortfall was less than if claiming early. Claiming early resulted in shortfalls in 29 percent of cases. Whenever the dots are above the diagonal line, the delayed claiming strategy with the HECM bridge provided a better result. This happens when legacy values are otherwise small or negative, which points to the risk management benefits of the strategy. It is only when net legacies are otherwise quite large that the delay strategy with the HECM bridge falls short. But legacies were still quite large either way. Risk averse retirees will tend to prefer strategies that provide more protection on the downside, even if that means sacrificing some upside. Exhibit 7.3 makes clear that this is the case for delaying Social Security and using the HECM as a delay bridge.

This analysis counters the suggestion from the CFPB that Social Security should not be delayed and a HECM should not be used to support the delay, at least for the characteristics in this case study. Except when markets do extremely well in retirement, the coordinated HECM strategy to build a delay bridge helps support a better financial outcome. It helps manage retirement risks. Contrary to conclusions made in the CFPB report, there is value in spending down other resources (either investments or home equity) during the first 8 years of retirement to enjoy a permanently higher Social Security benefit after that point. Using a HECM to fund Social Security delay does *not* create greater risk for retirees experiencing spending shocks or needing to move later in retirement, because reduced distribution needs from the investment portfolio and the aid this provides for reducing sequence risk offsets the HECM costs to better preserve overall net worth.

Exhibit 7.3
Comparing the Claim Social Security at 70 & HECM Delay Bridge
to the Claim Social Security at 62 and Use HECM as Last Resort
Net Real Legacies

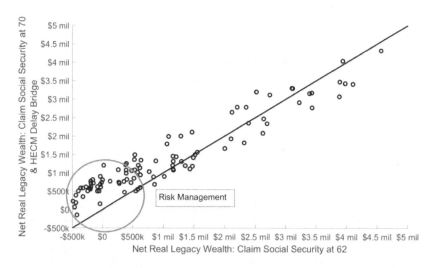

The HECM as a Resource to Manage Taxes

The case study in Chapter 5 used a distribution strategy from investments that was directionally correct for tax efficiency, but which may leave money on the table by not managing tax rates in the most effective manner. As a reminder, that strategy involved first taking any required minimum distributions from the tax-deferred account. If this, plus Social Security benefits and any distributions from the HECM, is less than the desired spending and income taxes due, additional withdrawals are then taken from the taxable account first until empty, then the tax-deferred account, and lastly the tax-free Roth account. Taxable assets create a drag on returns because taxes must be paid annually on interest and dividend payments. They are spent first while tax-advantaged accounts are given more opportunity to grow with tax deferral.

Regarding the case study introduced in Chapter 5, my effort to design an example that may be more representative for readers creates a situation where asset levels are not high enough to obtain large benefits from a Roth conversion strategy. With the last-resort strategy examined in Chapter 5, except for cases with strong market growth, the couple rarely left the 15 percent federal income tax bracket and did not generally have to pay taxes on long-term capital gains. There is not much room to reduce their tax rates, and so further tax planning can only take us so far. I found that using the HECM to pay taxes on a Roth conversion strategy can add value in the case study, but that this was more for the reasons related to portfolio coordination in Chapter 5 than for the benefits of a more tax-efficient spending strategy. Tax-efficient strategies work best when they can keep future distributions from experiencing higher tax rates, from triggering more tax on Social Security benefits, or from avoiding the need to pay higher Medicare premiums. These matters are not relevant with our case study.

The planning potential can be greatest when significant assets are held in tax-deferred accounts, such as IRAs. Those with around $2 million of investment assets may find more significant value from these tax planning strategies, so I will discuss how this can work.

Tax efficiency can be improved with a more blended strategy that mixes taxable and tax-deferred distributions at first, and then tax-deferred and tax-free distributions later, to provide more control over the adjusted gross income. A HECM could help by providing a resource to pay taxes on these strategies, which call for generating more taxes in the short-run to avoid even larger taxes in the long-run.

With tax planning, we recognize that taxes are unavoidable, but what we really seek to do is pay taxes at the lowest possible tax rates to generate the most lifetime spending and legacy power. This leads to opportunities to plan ahead within the progressive tax code that applies to annual income.

It is not just the federal income tax brackets we aim to manage. Taxable income can uniquely generate a need to pay taxes on more of Social Security benefits and can raise Medicare premiums. It can also trigger the net investment income surtax. After 2026, it may lead to phase-outs for personal exemptions and itemized deductions. In special cases, there could also be additional tax deductions and tax credits with income limits that could be lost. Front-loading some taxes in retirement may help prepare for better management of these pitfalls later in retirement.

In cases where spending needs have been met while additional capacity remains in a lower tax bracket, it may be worthwhile to fill that bracket with taxable income and pay tax at lower rates to help avoid the possibility of being pushed into a higher tax bracket in the future. This can be accomplished with Roth conversions, which take funds from qualified tax-deferred accounts and transfer them into a tax-exempt account. This triggers taxable income, because the deductible contributions and account gains are converted. By doing this strategically, the retiree can pay a lower tax rate on the converted amount and then have that money grow tax free in the future. This can help avoid paying higher tax rates on the assets in the future, especially after required minimum distributions begin.

The SECURE Act passed at the end of 2019 further increased the potential opportunities and value for Roth conversions. First, by raising the start age for required minimum distributions (RMDs) from 70.5 to 72, there is more opportunity and time to engage in Roth conversions before RMDs begin. Conversions can only be done on amounts that exceed the RMDs. The SECURE Act also changed the rules about RMDs for beneficiaries of retirement accounts, which may speed up the need for distributions from a lifetime stretch to a 10-year window. That could more easily force beneficiaries into higher tax brackets, especially if they are otherwise in their peak earnings years when receiving the inheritance.

Each retiree's situation is different. But one threshold that creates a big advantage for strategic management is the divide between the 12 percent and 22 percent tax brackets (which becomes a divide between 15 percent and 25 percent after 2026).

If there is spare capacity for taxable income in a lower tax bracket after meeting spending goals, the idea is to fill up the bracket with taxable income. We consider doing this by covering the spending needs from taxable accounts, then further increasing taxable income through Roth conversions with assets from the tax-deferred account, until the adjusted gross income reaches the desired target for the year. When doing these Roth conversions, raising taxable income also raises the tax bill, which can limit how much can be converted to the Roth account.

The HECM can provide a valuable resource to pay those taxes without generating a bigger tax bill, so that the greatest advantage can be obtained from the conversion. Conversely, when spending goals are pushing retirees into a higher than optimal level of taxable income, this process could work in the opposite direction, where distributions from tax-deferred sources could be reduced (with the caveat that RMDs must be met) and replaced with spending from sources that do not generate taxable income. Again, the HECM can provide retirees with a way to meet spending goals without pushing taxable income into a higher than necessary tax bracket or triggering other issues such as Social Security taxes or higher Medicare premiums. Having a resource to cover spending without generating taxable income can be very helpful for retirees who are actively attempting to manage their tax situation during retirement.

The Tenure Option as an Annuity Alternative

Using the HECM tenure payments as an alternative to purchasing an income annuity may be a consideration for those with an Income Protection or Risk Wrap retirement income style (see Chapter 1). The tenure option "annuitizes" home equity as an alternative to annuitizing financial assets. The tenure option behaves similarly to an income annuity in terms of providing a protected monthly income, but there are differences.

First, a tenure payment does not necessarily provide a guaranteed monthly cash flow for life, as an income annuity would. Guaranteed cash flow continues for as long as the borrower remains eligible for the loan by staying in the home and meeting homeowner obligations. This could be for life in some cases, but payments would stop as soon as the home is no longer the principal residence or if leaving the home for more than one year for medical reasons. While an eligible nonborrowing spouse may remain in the home if the borrower is no longer eligible, tenure payments stop once the borrower has become ineligible. Only when both spouses are eligible borrowers would the tenure payment behave like a joint-life annuity.

Another important difference is that no lump-sum payment (other than at least covering the mortgage counseling fee) must be given up from the investment portfolio to initiate the tenure payments. Each tenure payment is added to the loan balance as it is received. If the retiree dies early, the loan balance may be substantially less than an annuity premium would have been. Conceptually, the tenure payment behaves more closely to an income annuity with a cash-refund provision, in terms of whether any death benefit is available at the end of the contract period. Still, with the tenure option, there is no lump-sum premium to initiate these payments. This important distinction allows the tenure payment to further preserve investment assets.

The tenure payment also does not provide mortality credits in a conventional sense, though it does offer a type of mortality credit. Mortality credits are part of an income-annuity payment; they are the subsidies paid by the short-lived in the risk pool to the long-lived. Tenure-payment pricing assumes that the borrower or borrowers live to age 100. Despite the lack of traditional mortality credits, tenure payments provide a degree of longevity protection, assuming the borrower remains eligible. Cash flow received through the tenure payment can exceed the value of the principal limit and can even exceed the value of the home. This becomes more likely to happen as one lives longer. As I've noted, once this happens, the non-recourse aspects of the loan provide spending power without a trade-off to legacy—in a way, philosophically, like how an income annuity can continue to provide payments to the long-lived that well exceed the premium and earned interest. That non-recourse aspect could be interpreted as a type of mortality credit.

A final difference is between the formulas that calculate tenure payments and income-annuity payments. The tenure payout rate depends on the 10-year Treasury rate plus a lender's margin and a mortgage insurance premium rate of 0.5 percent. It also depends on an assumed time horizon or "life expectancy" of age 100. It does not vary by gender or whether payments are for one or two eligible borrowers. An income annuity, on the other hand, depends on actual mortality data for the age and gender of the individual or couple, as well as on a lower interest rate that may be a bit higher than a 10-year Treasury rate, because of its link to corporate bond yields; it doesn't include a lender's margin or mortgage insurance premium in its calculation.

About whether to choose tenure payments or income annuities, we can describe circumstances that would favor one or the other. First, as noted, couples and single females would experience lower payout rates from income annuities, as their pricing considers their increased longevity relative to single males. Single males can receive the highest relative payout rates from income annuities and would have a stronger reason to consider them, relatively speaking.

Second, tenure payments make more sense for those planning to remain in their homes, as they have more opportunity to spread out any upfront costs and potentially receive a windfall from the non-recourse aspect of tenure payments. For those likely to move or who otherwise do not live in an eligible home, income annuities have an edge.

Next, for those exhibiting a greater tolerance for risk, tenure payments are worth considering to obtain more guaranteed cash payments without having to take dollars out of the stock market. For income annuities, I suggest treating the annuitized assets as part of your bond holdings, but in practice this can be difficult. The remaining investment portfolio becomes more stock-heavy and volatile. In practice, real-world considerations probably mean that partial annuitization will also reduce stock holdings for most retirees, but the full portfolio and original asset allocation can remain intact more easily with tenure payments.

In a low-interest-rate environment, a given home value can support a higher tenure payment than otherwise. This gives tenure payments an advantage, providing more spending power for a given home-value-to-financial-portfolio ratio, relative to income annuities.

Finally, the tenure payments are not added to adjusted gross income, whereas annuity income is subject to taxes when initiated from either tax-deferred or taxable resources. Those facing higher potential tax rates on an annuity payment may prefer the tenure payment.

To summarize, tenure payments have many favorable characteristics. A tenure payment allows for an annuitized spending stream generated by home equity, subject to the caveat that it may not last for life if the borrower moves or cannot maintain the home. It does not require assets to be extracted as a large lump-sum annuity premium. For individuals uncomfortable with increasing their stock allocation for remaining assets after partial annuitization, the tenure payment option would allow more assets to remain in the stock market and focused on growth.

Chapter 8: Preserving Credit as "Insurance"

A final use for a HECM reverse mortgage is to preserve the line of credit as "insurance" against a variety of retirement risks. Preserving credit as insurance involves setting up a HECM reverse mortgage as early as possible and then leaving it unused until needed. The upfront costs for the reverse mortgage could be treated as an insurance premium that may never need to be used if everything else goes well in retirement.

However, a variety of potential pitfalls face retirees, and implementing a reverse mortgage earlier in retirement could support a sizeable pool of contingency assets to help manage unplanned expenses.

For example, the line of credit could be used to support in-home care or other health expenses to avoid or delay institutional living in the face of long-term-care needs. The line of credit could also be used as a resource for planned spending if investment assets are depleted. One might also use the line of credit as a source of cash flow to pay insurance premiums for existing long-term-care policies. With premium increases, these policies may become a bigger burden, and the HECM may provide a way to avoid lapsing the policy at an age where it may be needed most.

A reverse mortgage could also help as part of a divorce settlement. In this scenario, the reverse mortgage could allow one ex-spouse to stay in the home, with the reverse mortgage used to pay a necessary portion of the home's equity to the other ex-spouse. Alternatively, the home could be sold with the proceeds split, and then each of the ex-spouses could use his or her half of the home equity with a HECM for Purchase to obtain a home of similar value to the original.

The focus of this chapter is a final insurance aspect that requires a bit more explanation: using the HECM to protect the value of your home. With the current HECM rules, those living in their homes long enough could reap a windfall when the line of credit exceeds the home's value. Even if the value of the home declines, the line of credit will continue to grow without regard to the home's subsequent value.

Combining the principal limit with the fact that a HECM is a non-recourse loan means that the HECM provides a valuable hedging property for home prices. There is a chance that the line of credit value will grow to exceed the home value. We can investigate this possibility using the same historical data that has guided our simulations throughout the book. We use the same case study—a $450,000 home, a couple both age 62, a 2.5 percent lender's margin, and historical Treasury yields. Over rolling historical periods, we compare the evolving home price, growing at the rate of the Case-Shiller home price index, against the growing principal limit for a HECM loan initiated at age 62. Does the principal limit exceed the home value during the retirement horizon?

Exhibit 8.1 shows the probabilities that the HECM line of credit has grown to exceed the home's value for a 62-year-old borrower. With these simulations, there is a 50 percent chance this happens by age 90. If the upfront costs of $19,000 are financed into the loan, however, we see that the chance for a windfall net of costs will be 41 percent. These curves do not always increase with age; in the limited historical data, there are situations where home values suddenly appreciate to again rise above the principal limit after a period in which the principal limit was larger. Over time, though, we do observe a reasonable possibility that the HECM principal limit exceeds the home's value.

Exhibit 8.1
Probability that HECM Principal Limit Exceeds Home Value for 62-Year-Old

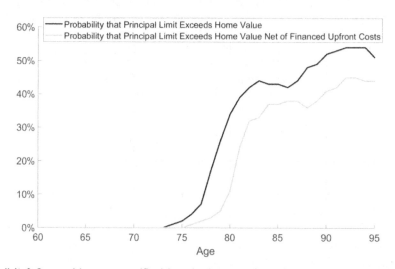

Exhibit 8.2 provides a specific historical example using the data starting in 1962. In this case, the principal limit rises above the home value in 1990, when the couple is 90 years old, creating the potential for a late-in-life windfall from an unused HECM credit line. Note, a *de minimis* $100 loan balance is required to keep the credit line open.

Exhibit 8.2
Comparing Home Value and Principal Limit, 1962-1995 Historical Data

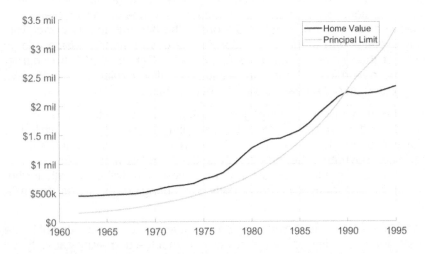

A few caveats for using this strategy to hedge home prices with the HECM are worth discussing. First, these probabilities may be underestimated, because any given home may experience more price volatility than the overall Case-Shiller national index. David Blanchett has estimated the volatility of individual homes at double the level of overall home price indexes used in these simulations. Individual homes are at more risk of experiencing substantial price declines relative to the index, creating more opportunity for the hedging value to be realized. The line of credit becomes valuable when the home price falls. In financial language, it is essentially a "put option" on the value of the home. The line of credit can provide a positive net payment when the home value declines. Put options are worth more when the price of the underlying asset they are attached to, which is your individual home, experiences greater volatility.

Second, there is an important aspect of timing the decision about when to access the line of credit. The longer you wait, the greater the potential growth for the pot of funds that can be obtained. Generally, the principal limit, loan balance, and line of credit grow at the same rate. But for any loan balance, the growth reflects the growing interest and mortgage premiums due rather than growing access to new funds. Waiting is advantageous, but if you wait too long and suddenly die, the line of credit is no longer available. Estates and nonborrowing spouses cannot take advantage of the windfall after the sudden death of the borrower. It is best not to become too greedy once a windfall has developed from this non-recourse aspect.

Finally, I must emphasize that this use of a HECM line of credit as home-value protection can be considered a "loophole" in the current program. Opening a reverse mortgage and then not using it works against the interests of some lenders and the government's mortgage insurance fund. The lender is not able to charge interest, which could create real difficulties for lenders that have reduced upfront costs by providing a higher margin and have paid a commission to the loan originator. Also, the mortgage insurance fund is unable to collect further premiums to support coverage of any shortfall to the lender when the borrower gets more out of the home than it is worth. This surely explains part of the justification for the government's closing a large portion of this "loophole" for loans issued after October 2017. It is harder under the new rules to benefit from this possibility. Exhibit 8.1 would have looked much more impressive with the earlier rules.

Borrowers may also be encouraged in subtle ways to let the value of their home decline so that they can make a smaller repayment. Thus, while this option is available today—and I could say that it is even encouraged with the heightened government efforts to reduce the speed at which borrowers use up their lines of credit—I expect that the government will eventually further weaken or eliminate this opportunity by changing the rules for new borrowers.

As new businesses are increasingly able to offer real-time estimates of home values, one possibility for future borrowers is that the borrowing capacity will be capped at the appraised home value. Another possibility is that the government could begin to charge the mortgage insurance premium on the value of the principal limit rather than on the loan balance. This would vastly increase the cost of the insurance strategy, possibly upending its value completely. However, for the time being, these insurance opportunities exist for those who initiate their loans under the current HECM rules.

Chapter 9: Determining if a HECM Reverse Mortgage is Right for You

In the previous chapters, I sought to provide context for how a retirement income strategy can extend beyond just investment management to better handle the many risks of retirement. Namely, I discussed a variety of ways that a strategic plan for home equity can improve retirement outcomes.

This final chapter is more about the process of deciding whether a HECM is right for you. I will answer some frequently asked questions I have received since publishing the first edition of this book. I'll also look in more detail at the risks associated with a reverse mortgage and provide tips on how to find a reverse mortgage lender. I will conclude with a summary of matters to keep in mind and a brief discussion about next steps for finding additional help or education on retirement topics.

Reverse Mortgage Risks

A common thought upon first learning about the HECM program is that it seems almost too good to be true and there must be a catch. I am often asked about reverse mortgage risks. I generally conclude that strategic HECM use can reduce overall retirement risks, but here I will summarize a few potential HECM risks to keep in mind.

Program Complexities Can Lead to Misunderstandings

When discussing risks for reverse mortgages, the first matter to emphasize is that many of the commonly mentioned risks involve misunderstandings on the part of borrowers or heirs about how the program works. In 2015, the Consumer Finance Protection Bureau published two reports about reverse mortgages that describe risks and complaints about the program. I know that these reports are getting old now, but they have not been updated and this is still the most recent information we have. First, their "Snapshot of Reverse Mortgage Complaints: December 2011–December 2014" was released in February 2015. It notes that for the 3-year period investigated, reverse mortgage complaints represent about 1 percent of the mortgage complaints received by the CFPB and that the reverse mortgage market size is about 1 percent of the total mortgage market. Thus, there is not a disproportionate number of complaints about reverse mortgages. Still, what are the complaints?

After reading this book, you should recognize that many of the complaints discussed in the CFPB report stem from misunderstandings on the part of those lodging them. Nonetheless, these complaints do allow us to reflect again on some of the complicated features of the HECM program and the misunderstandings they may generate. Double-check that these points are clear in your mind.

The most common complaint category relates to problems when someone is unable to achieve their aims, such as a borrower's desire to refinance a loan when home equity is insufficient to do so. Borrowers also complain about being unable to change loan terms, such as seeking to lower interest rates or the lender's margin, or feeling that the variable-rate portion of the effective rate has risen too quickly. Borrowers also complain about not being able to add additional borrowers to the loan so that they can avoid having the loan balance become due. For instance, adult children complain about not being able to be added to the loan as borrowers or at least as eligible nonborrowers. Nonborrowing spouses have complained about not being able to be added as borrowers after the loan commences.

Due to the actuarial nature of the program and how the principal limit factors are determined, it should be clear to readers that these types of requests are not allowed and not reasonable. Having more younger borrowers added to the loan would increase the time to loan maturity and would require a lower initial principal limit factor than already provided. As for nonborrowing spouses, the protections for eligible nonborrowing spouses were added near the end of the period under review (August 4, 2014), which should at least reduce these types of complaints. Nonborrowing spouses must remember, though, that they are not borrowers and will not be able to continue to access funds from the line of credit once the borrower leaves or dies.

In 2014, the Consumer Financial Protection Bureau conducted focus-group studies in which consumers were shown advertisements about reverse mortgages and asked for their perceptions. They provided the results of this investigation in a June 2015 report entitled, "A Closer Look at Reverse Mortgage Advertisements and Consumer Risks." Some of those in the focus group did not understand that a reverse mortgage would have to be repaid in the future, or that there are fees or interest involved. Rather, they viewed it as a government welfare program. Others viewed the loan balance as a way to spend home equity, not understanding the mechanism whereby this would reduce the value of their share of home equity in the future. Still others thought that the "tax-free" nature of reverse mortgages would mean that property taxes would no longer have to be paid. Others misunderstood how eligible nonborrowers must still meet the basic homeowner obligations to keep the right to stay in the home in the same manner as borrowers. I hope that this book will help clear up these misunderstandings.

FINRA's Stance on Reverse Mortgages

FINRA is the Financial Industry Regulatory Authority. It is a self-regulatory body for financial brokers and brokerage firms. As a part of its efforts to protect consumers, it issues alerts and reports on a variety of financial issues, including reverse mortgages. FINRA's stance on them is described in a report entitled, "Reverse Mortgages: Avoiding a Reversal of Fortune." This is a cute and clever title that clearly casts negative connotations on these mortgages, leading many financial advisors and financial broker-dealer firms who receive guidance from FINRA to conclude that reverse mortgages are a bad idea and do not allow their affiliated financial advisors to discuss reverse mortgages with their customers.

However, while its title has not changed, the report itself has evolved over the years. It used to tell investors to consider reverse mortgages only as a last-resort option, but after Barry Sacks published his research (discussed in Chapter 5), FINRA was convinced to remove that language.

The current version of the report provides three reasons to be cautious about reverse mortgages. Readers of Chapter 4 should be familiar with these matters. First, FINRA warns that reverse mortgages may "seem like 'free money' but in fact, they can be quite expensive." The report mentions the upfront costs and ongoing interest on the loan balance.

Second, the report mentions that reverse mortgages must be the primary mortgage on the home. This is not really a reason to be cautious, but the report points out that after paying off an existing mortgage from the initial principal limit, borrowers may have less access to cash in the credit line than they had anticipated.

Next, the report reminds investors that they are still responsible for property taxes, insurance, and home-maintenance costs.

Finally, the report reminds borrowers that the loan will become due should they decide to move out of the home. With accumulated interest, borrowers might be surprised about the amount of home equity that they have left after repaying the loan. The report then reminds borrowers to use the loan wisely rather than for frivolous expenses. As this book has focused on using home equity as part of a responsible retirement income plan, I hope this point is clear already.

The report ends with some tips for when you're considering reverse mortgages. First, weigh all your options. Besides a reverse mortgage, other options include selling one's house to downsize, using a home-equity line of credit, or seeking local-government assistance to help cover property taxes and home maintenance. Second, understand the costs and fees of the loan. Third, recognize the full impact of the reverse mortgage, including the potential impact on state and federal benefits such as Medicaid.

This section continues with the sentence, "Finally, a reverse mortgage is generally not the right choice for those who want to leave their homes to their heirs." However, this language should also have been removed, following the implications of the research outlined here. Since money is fungible, the report's statement is wrong. Coordinated strategies can create synergies for the investment portfolio to manage sequence risk that leads to a larger overall legacy after repaying any loan balance.

The next FINRA tip is to obtain independent advice through loan counseling, particularly if one is considering a proprietary reverse mortgage that is not part of the HECM program. Its last two points are about being skeptical about using reverse mortgages to fund an investment or insurance product. I have discussed coordinating the reverse mortgage with an existing portfolio or using a reverse mortgage to continue to pay premiums on an existing long-term-care policy, but I have not suggested that a HECM be used to fund new investments or insurance. This is taboo due to past abuses.

Dealing with the Loan-Servicing Companies

The one area that readers should remain wary about relates to loan servicing. Consumers have complained that servicers can make it difficult to coordinate repayment; may act as if property taxes and other homeowner obligations have not been met, in order to try to improperly foreclose on a loan; may not maintain accurate records (or even lose important documents); and are unresponsive to communications. Furthermore, when the loan balance comes due, some have complained of appraisers inflating home values to force a higher payoff amount. Since the loan balance continues to grow with interest until repayment is made, delays in this area have the effect of increasing the subsequent amount due.

One example I have personally witnessed is of a reader who obtained a reverse mortgage and then experienced hail damage to the roof of the home. The homeowner's insurance provided a check to repair the roof but made it out to both the homeowner and the reverse mortgage servicing company. The reverse mortgage servicer was unresponsive about endorsing the check so that it could be cashed and the roof could be repaired.

Fortunately, in this case, the reverse mortgage lender who had initiated the loan stepped in and worked with the servicer to make sure that the right actions were taken. The lender was not obligated to help with this. This may indicate how working with someone locally (rather than remotely, through a call center) can be important for getting help with future servicing issues. It may be worth paying a bit more in upfront costs to work with someone who can serve as a trustworthy advocate. Choosing a servicer for a reverse mortgage is no guarantee, though, because just like with traditional mortgages, these loans are traded, and you may end up with a different servicer than you expect.

Temptations to Use Irresponsibly

Another risk for reverse mortgages relates to the fact that spending down home equity does mean that less of it will be available later in retirement. Of course, this is also true with an investment portfolio, but people seem to frame the issue differently with home equity. Any outstanding loan balance on a reverse mortgage grows with interest over time. Borrowers must understand this point.

Creating liquidity for home equity with a reverse mortgage can allow for more strategic planning that better protects against sequence-of-return risk for portfolio distributions. But there is always a temptation to overspend when the money is available. For those who might look at a reverse mortgage as an opportunity to overspend, this could jeopardize the ability to meet spending obligations later in retirement. Such individuals may be better off keeping their home equity illiquid and thereby avoid misusing their nest egg.

For those who incorporate reverse mortgages as part of a responsible overall plan and do not use the home equity on unnecessary luxuries, this risk is not relevant. But it remains a risk for those without adequate self-control.

Qualifying for Means-Tested Benefits

Proceeds from a reverse mortgage can be described as "tax free" in the sense that these cash flows do not count as part of the adjusted gross income for determining income taxes. However, spending from a reverse mortgage, or holding some reverse mortgage proceeds in a bank account, could reduce eligibility for means-tested benefits such as Supplemental Security Income or Medicaid. For those thinking about reverse mortgages as a last-resort option, it is important to consider the potential impact of the reverse mortgage on other government benefits.

Destruction of the Home through Natural Disasters

A common question I receive relates to what happens to the reverse mortgage if a home is destroyed through earthquake, flood, fire, and the like. Generally, the homeowner has sufficient insurance coverage to rebuild the home on the same property, and the disaster event will not trigger the loan balance to become due. However, the loan balance could become due if one has insufficient insurance coverage to rebuild, or decides to move to a new location because it is impossible to rebuild on the same property.

The risk here is that the loan balance could become due sooner than the borrower had expected. For those with sufficient remaining assets, this could be a nuisance but not necessarily a severe disruption for the success of the retirement plan.

But this risk can be particularly problematic for those using a reverse mortgage as a last-resort option. An extreme example of this risk took place in Oregon in 2012, when a woman in her 80s had her home taken through eminent domain to allow a highway expansion through her area. The woman had already spent the proceeds from the reverse mortgage and had enough income to continue maintaining the obligations to stay in her home. But while the eminent-domain action compensated her for the value of the home, the money had to be used to repay the loan balance on the reverse mortgage, because she could no longer live on the property. In this case, the unexpected need to repay the reverse mortgage loan because of the eminent-domain action essentially left her homeless. Any natural disaster that requires a move from the original property could create the same impact. This does have to be considered a risk.

For those without other options, it is important to consider what the alternatives would have been without the reverse mortgage. While the situation is bad when one can unexpectedly no longer live in the home, this type of outcome might simply have occurred even earlier in the absence of the reverse mortgage. With this risk, it is not clear that a reverse mortgage was a bad idea, unless it was being used simply to fund frivolous expenses. It is a tough situation, though, and perhaps an area that warrants further consumer protections.

The Maximum Mortgage Amount

Reverse mortgage contracts need inherent limits on how long they last and on how much can be borrowed. They cannot be limitless. The higher the limits, the higher the demand on the mortgage insurance fund and the larger the payments for the mortgage insurance premiums. In states where these limits must be specified, the constraints are generally to age 150 and to a maximum mortgage amount of 150 percent of the eligible home value when the HECM begins. For instance, if a home is appraised at $600,000 when initiating the HECM, then the maximum mortgage amount is $900,000.

Though borrowers are unlikely to find the age limit binding, it is possible for the principal limit to grow to the size of the maximum mortgage amount. This happened quite frequently in our historical simulations. What happens when the principal limit reaches this limit?

The consensus within the reverse mortgage industry is that lenders will allow the borrower to sign paperwork to modify the loan documents to further extend the maximum mortgage amount, ensuring that the disbursements from the line of credit can continue even if it would push the loan balance above the maximum mortgage amount set in the original contract. Though it will be necessary to revisit the reverse mortgage with additional paperwork at that time, the common expectation is that lenders will be willing to coordinate the allowance of further disbursements from the loan beyond the original limit. This is what I assumed in the book's case studies.

It should be noted that not everyone in the reverse mortgage world expects this to proceed so smoothly. For those whose principal limit includes a substantial loan-balance component, the process is likely to operate as anticipated. But a caveat should be made for those considering the "ruthless option" for the reverse mortgage, which is the option to open a reverse mortgage line of credit and then let it sit unused for decades, with the hope that one day the line of credit will grow larger than the value of the home and provide a windfall due to the loan's non-recourse aspects. It is plausible that, in such cases, lenders will be unwilling to modify the loan documents, which could mean that disbursements from the line of credit cannot exceed the maximum mortgage amount. If this happens, the line of credit's growth would remain capped at 150 percent of the eligible home value when the loan began, rather than continuing without any limit. This should be viewed as a potential risk for those who open a HECM line of credit and leave it unused for decades.

Finding a High-Quality Reverse Mortgage Lender

Another common question I receive regards how to find a trustworthy reverse mortgage lender. This is not necessarily easy for those beginning the process with little more to rely on than an Internet search engine. A starting point may be with personal referrals from your financial advisor, or from friends or family who have felt satisfied with their lenders.

It is important to speak with a few different lenders and get a sense of the range of options in terms of upfront costs, the lender's margin, ongoing costs, and whether the lender can serve as a resource to address any servicing issues after the loan is initiated. Costs will vary and can depend on how the loan is used: Those wishing to set up a line of credit as a later resource may have to pay a higher upfront cost than those who plan to spend more quickly from the HECM, such as by refinancing an existing mortgage. It is important to consider more than just who offers the lowest upfront costs, because having a personal connection to the lender can be important for any subsequent servicing issues or questions, and because the interaction of upfront costs and the lender's margin can be hard to assess.

Here are some issues to consider when speaking with a lender:

- Is the lender patient about meeting with you in person or speaking by phone to answer your questions?
- Is the lender clear about the different terms and costs available for reverse mortgages? Does he or she explain the costs clearly and not just wave them away by emphasizing "no out-of-pocket" costs?
- Has the lender been clear about your responsibilities regarding property taxes, maintaining homeowner's insurance, and keeping the property maintained?
- Has the lender suggested that you seek additional guidance for tax advice or for advice about receiving assistance from government-welfare programs, if relevant?
- Does the lender demonstrate interest or knowledge about retirement income planning so that you have a better sense about the right options and strategies for your situation? Is the lender conversant about the topics and issues raised in this book?

In addition, here are red flags that may suggest looking for a different lender:

- The lender pressures you to decide about applying for a reverse mortgage before you feel comfortable or ready.
- The lender encourages you to take a larger proceed from the line of credit when the loan begins than you feel is necessary.
- The lender encourages you to use the reverse mortgage proceeds to buy an investment or insurance product, especially if it seems as though the lender could receive additional compensation if you do.
- The lender provides you with a list of HUD-approved independent counselors, as they should, but tries to direct you to a specific counselor on the list.

Final Thoughts on Reverse Mortgages

We have covered a lot of ground. I first introduced retirement income planning and the new risks of retirement to provide a context and framework for thinking about how home equity could be integrated into a retirement income strategy. I then described the variable-rate HECM option in detail and provided case studies using historical data to understand how different HECM uses impact a retirement plan in terms of retaining a legacy after meeting a lifetime spending goal. I showed the potential value in incorporating HECMs early on as part of an overall strategy rather than treating housing wealth as a last-resort asset for retirement. I then considered the risks to keep in mind about reverse mortgages and some tips for finding a good lender.

At present, reverse mortgages are underutilized by the US population. Mark Warshawsky, a senior fellow at the American Enterprise Institute, reports that in 2015 there were about 36 million US households with someone age 62 or older, and roughly 1.6 percent of them were using HECMs. He estimates, however, that about 12 percent to 14 percent of these households were suitable candidates for HECMs: Their homes were eligible, they had mortgages of less than 40 percent of the home's value, and they could generate at least 10 percent more overall retirement income with a HECM.

There is still plenty of room for growth with the HECM program.

If you are thinking of using a reverse mortgage in retirement, it is important to first ensure that you are eligible. Is a potential borrower at least 62? Is the home used as the primary residence? Do you plan on living in the home for at least long enough to make it worthwhile to pay the upfront costs for setting up the reverse mortgage? Is there an existing mortgage on the home that is small enough to be paid off with other assets and/or refinanced through the credit available with the reverse mortgage? Do you understand the details of how reverse mortgages work as well as the costs and homeowner obligations? Is there another strategy, such as downsizing your home, that might be better for you? Do you have a strategy in mind for how the reverse mortgage could improve your financial outcomes? Have you discussed your plan with your children or other beneficiaries, so that they understand the loan repayment process?

My hope is that this book will help you structure answers to these questions, especially regarding how you intend to use the reverse mortgage.

Financial Advisors and Fiduciary Duty

Financial advisors should strive to work toward the best interests of their clients. But many financial firms prohibit their advisors from discussing how to incorporate housing wealth within their clients' retirement plans. For the average American household, housing wealth represents about 2/3 of the overall asset base, making this is a dramatic oversight. This book demonstrates how thoughtful coordination of a HECM into a retirement plan creates a strong likelihood of improving financial outcomes for retirees and specifically helps to manage the risk of being unable to meet financial goals. It is my hope that these findings can contribute to further discussions that improve the understanding and value of tools such as reverse mortgages to help manage retirement risk. Then more financial firms will be open to the possibility of discussing housing wealth as part of the retirement planning process. With financial planning, it is difficult to serve the best interests of clients if one is unable to consider all available household assets.

Opportunities for Further Engagement

As we finish, please let me outline a few ways to continue engaging together. First you can visit **www.RetirementResearcher.com** and sign up for our weekly email newsletter with our latest articles, invitations to webinars, Q&A sessions, and more. The newsletter arrives each Saturday morning.

Alex Murguia and I also host the *Retire with Style* podcast, which is available through most podcast platforms. If you are interested to dive deeper into retirement income topics, I also suggest checking out my *Retirement Planning Guidebook*.

As well, I created Retirement Researcher as a blog in September 2010. As it developed, I tried to maintain the original mission to provide independent, data-driven, and research-based information about retirement income planning. The website is geared toward providing unbiased information about building efficient retirement income strategies and endeavors to bridge the various retirement income styles.

Our most recent innovation regarding this bridging is the Retirement Income Style Awareness I described in Chapter 1. If you are interested in obtaining your RISA Profile as an initial step toward retirement income planning, you can do so without cost at **www.risaprofile.com/reverse** .

We also offer the Retirement Researcher Academy membership site for self-directed retirees. The Academy empowers members with a clearinghouse of knowledge to take the best of what is empirically valid in a cohesive manner and digest at your own pace and as needed. Retirement Researcher also provides opportunities to work with its sister firm, McLean Asset Management (**www.mcleanam.com**). McLean offers various one-time planning options as well as ongoing wealth management. I can help you arrange an introductory call to learn more about these options (**wade@retirementresearcher.com**).

Make an Author Happy!

If you found this information helpful, I would truly appreciate it if you left a brief review of the book at your favorite book retailer. Perhaps you could mention the most useful item you learned. As the book is self-published, it can be a challenge to get the word out to a wider audience and every review helps to get this information in front of more readers. Thank you!

Further Reading

AARP. 2020. *AARP HomeFit Guide.* Available at https://www.aarp.org/livable-communities/housing/info-2020/homefit-guide.html

Accola, Harlan J. 2018. Home Equity and Reverse Mortgages: The Cinderella of the Baby Boomer Retirement. Marshfield, WI: A Better Way to Live.

Blanchett, David. 2017. "The Home as a Risky Asset." *Journal of Personal Finance* 16 (1): 7–28.

Center for Retirement Research at Boston College. 2014. *Using Your House for Income in Retirement.*

Coughlin, Joseph F. 2013. "3 Questions Predict Future Quality of Life." *MarketWatch RetireMentors Series* (April 17).

Consumer Financial Protection Bureau. 2017. "Issue Brief: The Costs and Risks of Using a Reverse Mortgage to Delay Collecting Social Security."

Consumer Financial Protection Bureau. 2015. "Snapshot of Reverse Mortgage Complaints; December 2011–December 2014."

Consumer Financial Protection Bureau. 2015. "A Closer Look at Reverse Mortgage Advertisements and Consumer Risks."

Consumer Finance Protection Bureau. 2014. "Snapshot of Older Consumers and Mortgage Debt."

Financial Industry Regulatory Authority. 2014. "Reverse Mortgages: Avoiding a Reversal of Fortune." Investor Education Series.

Giordano, Shelley. 2019. *What's the Deal with Reverse Mortgages? (2nd Edition).* Rethink Press.

Graves, Don. 2018. *Housing Wealth: An Advisor's Guide to Reverse Mortgages.* Philadelphia, PA: Housing Wealth Institute.

Green, Richard. 2013. "Who Moves? Not Old People." *Forbes* (July 23).

Hultquist, Dan. 2023. *Understanding Reverse – 2023.* Canton, GA: Independently Published.

Merrill Lynch and AgeWave. 2015. "Home in Retirement: More Freedom, New Choices."

National Council on Aging. 2021. "Use Your Home to Stay at Home."

Pfau, Wade D. 2021. Retirement Planning Guidebook: Navigating the Important Decisions for Retirement Success. Vienna, VA: Retirement Researcher Media.

Pfeiffer, Shaun, John R. Salter, and Harold R. Evensky. 2013. "Increasing the Sustainable Withdrawal Rate Using the Standby Reverse Mortgage." *Journal of Financial Planning* 26 (12): 55–62.

Sacks, Barry H., Nicholas Miningas, Stephen R. Sacks, and Francis Vitagliano. 2016. "Recovering a Lost Deduction." *Journal of Taxation* 124 (4): 157–169.

Sacks, Barry H., and Stephen R. Sacks. 2012. "Reversing the Conventional Wisdom: Using Home Equity to Supplement Retirement Income." *Journal of Financial Planning* 25 (2): 43–52.

Salter, John R., Shaun A. Pfeiffer, and Harold R. Evensky. 2012. "Standby Reverse Mortgages: A Risk Management Tool for Retirement Distributions." *Journal of Financial Planning* 25 (8): 40–48.

Urban Institute. 2021. "Mortgage Denial Rates and Household Finances Among Older Americans." Urban Institute Research Report (October).

US Department of Housing and Urban Development. 2021. *FHA Single Family Production Report*.

US Department of Housing and Urban Development also provides details on HECM rules and contact information for housing counselors at www.hud.gov.

Wagner, Gerald C. 2013. "The 6.0 Percent Rule." *Journal of Financial Planning* 26 (12): 46–54.

Warshawsky, Mark J. 2018. "Retire on the House: The Possible Use of Reverse Mortgages to Enhance Retirement Security." *Journal of Retirement* 5:3 (Winter): 10-31.

The Retirement Researcher's Guide Series

The Retirement Researcher's Guide Series includes four volumes. The other three volumes provide a deeper dive into various aspects of retirement planning. These books are available at most major retailers. I can also arrange discounted bulk orders for any of the four volumes in this series. Please contact me about bulk orders at **wade@retirementresearcher.com**.

Retirement Planning Guidebook	*How Much Can I Spend in Retirement?*	*Safety-First Retirement Planning*
A deep dive into all the important decisions needed for a comprehensive retirement plan.	A deeper exploration of strategies for those with total return and time segmentation styles.	A deeper exploration of strategies for those with income protection and risk wrap styles.

Index

About the Author

Wade D. Pfau, PhD, CFA, RICP® is the founder of Retirement Researcher, an educational resource for individuals and financial advisors on topics related to retirement income planning. He is a co-founder of the Retirement Income Style Awareness tool and a co-host of the *Retire with Style* podcast. He also serves as a principal and the director of retirement research for McLean Asset Management. He also serves as a Research Fellow with the Alliance for Lifetime Income and Retirement Income Institute. He is a professor of practice at the American College of Financial Services and past director of the Retirement Income Certified Professional® (RICP®) designation program.

He holds a doctorate in economics from Princeton University and has published more than sixty peer-reviewed research articles in a wide variety of academic and practitioner journals. His research has been discussed in outlets including the print editions of the *Economist, New York Times, Wall Street Journal, Time, Kiplinger's,* and *Money* magazine.

Wade is a past selectee for the *InvestmentNews* Power 20 in 2013 and inaugural 40 Under 40 in 2014, the Investment Advisor 35 list for 2015 and 25 list for 2014, and *Financial Planning* magazine's Influencer Awards. In 2016, he was chosen as one of the Icons and Innovators by *InvestmentNews*. He is a two-time winner of the *Journal of Financial Planning* Montgomery-Warschauer Editor's Award, a two-time winner of the Academic Thought Leadership Award from the Retirement Income Industry Association, and a Best Paper Award winner in the Retirement category from the Academy of Financial Services. Wade served for four years as a coeditor of the *Journal of Personal Finance.*

Wade is a contributor to *Forbes* and an Expert Panelist for the *Wall Street Journal*. He has spoken at the national conferences of organizations such as the CFA Institute, the CFP Board, the FPA, NAPFA, and the Academy of Financial Services.

He is also author of three other books in the Retirement Researcher's Guide Series, *Retirement Planning Guidebook: Navigating the Important Decisions for Retirement Success, How Much Can I Spend in Retirement: A Guide to Investment-Based Retirement Income Strategies,* and *Safety-First Retirement Planning: An Integrated Approach for a Worry-Free Retirement.*

Twitter: @WadePfau

Website: RetirementResearcher.com

Contact: wade@retirementresearcher.com

Made in United States
Orlando, FL
13 January 2024

42480229R00078